Art Textiles of the World:
Australia

TELOS

Edited by Matthew Koumis

Reprographics by StudioTec, Leeds

Printed by Steffprint, Keighley, West Yorkshire

© Telos Art Publishing 1999

First published in Great Britain, 1999

ISBN 0 9526267 0 5

A CIP catalogue record for this book is available from the British Library

Telos Art Publishing
PO Box 125, Winchester SO23 7UJ
England
Facsimile: ++ 44 (0)1962 864 727
www.telos.net

Cover illustrations
front and back:
Jeannie Petyarre
Alhalkere Dreaming (detail)
batik on silk
photograph by Barry Allwright

back:
Patricia Black
Ferrous Extrusion (detail)
silk organza, shibori techniques
photograph by Eardley Lancaster

Photography Credits
Barry Allwright pp14,15,16,18,20 John Austin p22, Patricia Black p81, Tony Boyd pp12,63, Michael Coates pp5,38,39,42, John Farrow p92, Victor France pp25,58, Bret Geague p34, Leslie Goldacre pp62,66,68,69, Chiara Goya p65, Barrie Hadlow p87, Ian Hobbs pp41,44, Stuart Humphreys p78, Henry Jolles p75, Ricardo Martin p79, Neal McCracken Anu Photography pp11,71,76, Brenton McGeachi p30, Stuart Owen Fox pp9,31,33,36,37, Richard Parkinson pp10,86,89,90,91, David Paterson p70, Jean Pierre p85, Ashley de Prazer pp7,23,26,28 Queen Victoria Museum and Art Gallery, Tasmania p73, Jan Ross Manley p21, Bill Shaylor pp3,54,55,57,60, Dr John Storey pp8,46,47,48,51,52,53, Dean Tirkot pp82,84.

Pam Gaunt
Hearts on a Sleeve (1997) (detail)
photocopied draughting film,
fabric, thread, labels etc
machine embroidery
1240 x 620 mm

Contents

Editor's Foreword

Making any selection of artists and their work is a difficult undertaking. Before drawing up a shortlist for *Art Textiles of the World: Australia* I spoke widely and informally with a broad range of Australian artists and viewed extensively the slide banks of the State Crafts Councils. I also consulted a number of leading curators including Grace Cochrane of the Powerhouse Museum, Sydney, Robert Bell of the Art Gallery of Western Australia, Professor Sue Rowley of the College of Fine Arts, University of New South Wales, Sydney, and Janet De Boer of The Australian Forum for Textile Arts.

The final choice of artists, however, is mine. I believe the selection in this volume offers the reader an impression of the diversity, sensitivity and courage of contemporary Australian textile artists. My mission as editor is to make a personal and varied selection not for an exhibition but for a two-dimensional book. On occasions, and with regret, an artist has been excluded where the quality of photographic transparencies was not sufficiently high to do their work justice. It has never been my intention to produce a 'Top Ten', even if such a list were achievable, and several prominent artists have been deliberately held over, to be invited to appear in a second volume in due course.

Three themes stand out clearly in this present volume, the first being the land; second is the movement of people to and around the land — indeed the land could be said to be the subject of this book as much as textiles. Third is the body and its adornment.

The work of the Aboriginal community at Utopia may need a few words of introduction. The name Utopia is somewhat ironic for such a difficult desert terrain some 250 kilometres north of Alice Springs. The artists whose work is illustrated here, Gloria Petyarre, Jeannie Petyarre, Ada Bird Petyarre, Nora Petyarre, Old Polly Gnale, Amy Napangardi and Lena Pwerle, live in family clans where they are able to devote much of their time to their art work, be it body-painting, sand-painting, batik on silk or painting on canvas. While the community has become celebrated internationally, the names of the individual artists are little known, and the women prefer not to be singled out for individual recognition. The batik work portrays motifs of the Dreaming, the Aboriginal concept of creation. An artist will be entrusted with a particular image, be it an animal such as a lizard, or a specific terrain. It is seen as their sacred obligation to reproduce this motif visually their whole life long.

Amy Napangardi
Untitled (1996)
silk satin, batik
1.2 x 3 m

Other artists devoting much of their work to a subtle dialogue with the land include Ruth Hadlow, Jan Irvine-Nealie, Elsje van Keppel and Tori de Mestre. The earth's vulnerability, fragility and capacity to nurture are suggested with expressive nuance, often through the resourceful inclusion of materials such as spinifex, guinea-fowl feathers, river stone, eucalypt sticks and paperbark.

The second recurring theme is migration. Valerie Kirk's tapestries are an example of a dialogue with the land by one who has relatively recently arrived in the country, while the weavings of Chilean-born Elena Gallegos reverberate with the trauma of exile. Patrick Snelling's *Crossing Borders* series exemplify an open-minded embrace of new technologies with the immigrant's quest for identity. His pattern-making offers a link to the third recurring theme, that of the body: Pam Gaunt's work explores pattern-making in the context of gallery installations, while Patricia Black is an outstanding exponent of the burgeoning wearable art movement sweeping Australia and New Zealand.

Visiting Australia was an unforgettable privilege and joy. I blame everyone I met for kindling in me a hugely inconvenient urge to move to Australia. I should also thank the artists for their boundless patience and trust, and the many people who offered their encouragement, advice, assistance, hospitality and generosity during research for this book, including Robert Bell, Eugenie Keefer Bell, Grace Cochrane, Ann Guild, Steve Harken, Josephine Heitter at Craft Australia, Lyn Inall, Liz Jeneid, Jean Kropper, Jan Ross-Manley, Marco Marcon, Sharon Peebles, Celia Player, Emma Robertson, Sue Rowley, Annette Seaman, Sue Trytell, Gabriella Verstraeten, Liz Williamson and many others. A special thank you to Janet De Boer, Kristen Dibbs and Anne Marie Power. In addition I wish to thank two artists from New Zealand, the Maori weaver Puti Rare and the designer of wearable art Susan Holmes, whom I had hoped to include in this volume — it was later considered preferable to wait for a future volume where more space could be devoted to them and to others from New Zealand — thanks meanwhile to Freda Brierley and to writer and ethnologist Mick Pendergrast of the Auckland Institute and Museum for their expertise and assistance. In England I wish to thank Margie Barton, Viv Brett, David Eno, Edward Fennell, David Kay and Keiren Phelan of Southern Arts, David Lawless and Paul Markham at Studio Tec, Paul Richardson of Oxford Brookes University, George Wilkinson and all at Steffprint, Laurence and Augusta Wolff, and my wife Alice for her patient support.

This book is dedicated to my Mother and Father.

Enjoy!

Jan Irvine Nealie
Wishing on the Rain (1997) (detail)
airbrush dyed silk, wool fill
hand-stitched
78 x 98 cm

1. Pam Gaunt, Elsje van Keppel (Perth, WA)
2. Utopia Awely Batik Aboriginal Corporation (near Alice Springs NT)
3. Patrick Snelling (Melbourne, Victoria)
4. Ruth Hadlow (Hobart,Tasmania)
5. Valerie Kirk (Canberra, ACT)
6. Tori de Mestre (Wollongong, NSW)
7. Patricia Black (Sydney)
8. Jan Irvine-Nealie (Gulgong, NSW)
9. Elena Gallegos (Byron Bay, NSW)

Elsje van Keppel
in the making (1996) (detail)
wool fabric, linen thread,
resist dyed, vegetable dyed,
hand stitched

Gaining Momentum:

Diversity and dialogue in contemporary Australian textiles

Contemporary textiles and fibre art in Australia has reached critical mass. Current exhibitions bring together diverse practices into confident, coherent shows. Craftspractitioners, artists and designers from many cultural backgrounds are inspired by connections and differences they perceive in the work of colleagues. Many of today's senior artists have been nurtured by generations of domestic embroidery, quilting, knitting and sewing; and many were trained by artists who were themselves educated as professional textile artists here and overseas. Emerging artists, recently graduating from university and TAFE (technical and further education) art and design schools, anticipate working as designers and artists, producing both exhibition work and 'production' textiles for retail and industry prototypes. Curators and writers, drawn not only from within the domain of craft and decorative arts, but broadly from many disciplines (design, visual art, literature and film theory, cultural studies & cultural history, and so on), supplement the work of artists. National, state and regional art museums have collected and exhibited Australian textiles and fibre art, and a number of outstanding curators have played a vital educative role in the broader crafts communities. There is a dynamic and committed infrastructure of crafts organisations, public arts bodies, textile artists' networks, galleries, journals, retail outlets and studios.

Undoubtedly, integrating Indigenous and non-indigenous art is the major fulcrum in any comprehensive account — whether in the form of exhibitions, collections, or publications — of Australian contemporary textiles at present. Not so long ago, indigenous fibre work might well have been positioned as a 'pre-history to European settlement', emphasising a continuous history that reaches back 40,000 years and more. Such accounts have tended to eclipse elements of cultural exchange and personal innovation in traditional culture and have tended to ignore the on-going practice and evolution of Indigenous art in the nineteenth and twentieth centuries. Now, the notion of 'contemporary' embraces textiles and fibre work made by Indigenous artists, including those living in comparatively isolated communities, and maintaining traditional cultures through the making and using of these artefacts.

Tracing the history of Indigenous fibre culture certainly embraces the difference ways of organising time and space that shape Aboriginal cultures, imparting a deep sense of temporal continuity and a profound connection with ancestral country and culture. Doreen Mellor, an Indigenous curator and the Director of The Flinders University Art Museum, describes fibre as 'an essential element of value systems relating to the most profound aspects of human activity — that of spiritual experience and the ceremony which expresses it'. She identifies two characteristic 'modalities': 'the use of form and its intrinsic rhythms as a powerful and unaccompanied aesthetic element; and the use of colour or materials other than that provided by the fibre itself, applied or attached to its surfaces as a way to enhance it and embody layers of meaning'. Maningrida and Ngarrindjeri basketmakers exemplify the first category. Batik artists from the Ernabella and Utopia communities, including Old Polly Gnale, Lena Pwerle, Jeannie Petyarre and Amy Napangardi, fit into the second category. Noting that 'the prevalence of one or the other of these two ways of working is usually related to place and cultural alignment', she also observes 'within the self-imposed boundaries of cultural alliance, individual fibre practitioners exercise their options for creative self-expression and choice of approach'. [1]

Personal self-expression and artistic choice within shared systems of cultural value and meaning were and are characteristic of Indigenous art, every bit as much as it is of the Euro-American traditions of visual art. This perspective challenges a tendency to over-state the extent of personal authorship in the western traditions, and provides the critical and cultural understanding for recognising individual artistic expression and innovation in non-western cultures.

Consistent with this notion of personal innovation within traditional culture is an openness of response to cultural exchange. Cultural exchange with traders and seafarers from South East Asia pre-dates European settlement in the north of the continent. Much of the dynamic contemporary textile art from Indigenous communities integrates traditional cultures with techniques, imported materials and hybrid aesthetics, adopted from a range of other cultures including other Aboriginal cultures, from Indonesia and from Anglo-European Australian culture. For example, coiled basketry of south Australian Ngarrindjeri people was introduced to Maningrida, in the Northern Territory, at the turn of the century by missionary Gretta Matthew. *Two Countries, One Weave*, a 1991 exhibition curated by Kerry Giles, celebrated the basketry of Maningrida and Ngarrindjeri people who are renowned for contemporary basket-making. Maningrida artists retain an unbroken link with their ancient culture, and produce traditional artefacts and innovative forms. Basket-making, along with other cultural forms including language, was all but lost to Ngarrindjeri people, but has been revitalised since the early 1980s by Ellen Trevorrow and Yvonne Koolmatrie.

What is distinctive about the integration of Indigenous work into the domain of contemporary practice is the irrelevance of the art-craft issue which remains unresolvable in the Euro-American traditions which continue to shape the non-Indigenous interpretative and evaluative frameworks for non-indigenous textiles. For example, the Australian exhibition in the *1997 47th Venice Biennale*, titled *Fluent*, showed the work of three indigenous artists, Emily Kane Kngwarreye, Yvonne Koolmatrie and Judy Watson. [2] Emily Kane Kngwarreye, a senior woman in the remote Utopia community, was introduced to non-traditional practices through the batik exchanges with Indonesia, before turning to painting on canvas. Sydney-based artist Judy Watson has achieved international recognition for her subtle pigment-washed and chalk-drawn canvases which use the Euro-American traditions in which she has trained to tell the stories of colonisation and reclaim history and her Waanyi identity. Ngarrindjeri artist Yvonne Koolmatrie uses basket-making in both innovative and traditional forms. Ironically perhaps, her traditional forms, such as her lyrical eel traps, have been exhibited in major art exhibitions including the *1997 Venice Biennale* and *Australian Perspecta 1993*, while her most individual expressions of personal narrative and innovative forms have been developed for textiles exhibitions such as *Below the Surface* (1996) and *Weave* (1998). These artists, as curator Hetti Perkins notes, test the parameters, contest boundaries and override the cultural constructions of hierarchical difference in Indigenous and non-indigenous, traditional and contemporary art traditions, including those relating to art and craft.

This overriding of imaginary distinctions, at least by Indigenous practitioners and curators, has profoundly inflected current Australian textiles practice. It comes as a shock to recall that this decisive impact has registered only quite recently, really since the mid 1990s.

Patrick Snelling
Perfect People Print (1995) (detail)
screen-printed pigmented and
heat-sensitised inks, acid-dyed silk,
machine-stitched and appliqued on
cotton and linen cloth, buttons
137 x 231 cm

Gillian McCracken, curator of the *13th Tamworth Fibre Textile Biennial* in 1998, included Indigenous practice as one of four 'territories of influence'. Other major strands nominated were 'textile practices which established a domestic, formative environment throughout our long history; northern European influences of the 1960s and 1970s which generated experimentation in scale and sculptural form as well as defining textile practice as "professional"; an attitudinal shift for Australian women practitioners; and contemporary exchange with many Asian cultures'. [3]   Gillian McCracken rightly emphasises the formative role of migration and multi-culturalism in shaping textile practice in Australia.

The post-war immigration of trained artisans and designers was formative in the shaping of Australian textiles, seeding a sophisticated modernist formalism in design and virtuosity in execution, particularly in weaving and tapestry. A significant impetus was given to the emerging Australian craft 'movement' in the 1950s by the formation of the Sturt workshops in 1941. From the 1950s, a succession of European, Scandinavian and Japanese weavers have left their imprint on the culture of professionalism within the crafts, which has become quite strikingly evident again in recent years. The integration of modern design and hand-production, and the values placed on aesthetic qualities, the materiality of objects, inventiveness and rigorous standards of technical skill, may have been somewhat eclipsed in rhetorical 'art/craft' debates of the 1980s. But they inform a wide spectrum of practices in textiles today.

Artisan practices and apprenticeship training, combined with Bauhaus-influenced philosophies and work practices, offered a sense of order and purpose to artists leaving unsettled, sometimes devasted European homes to take up new opportunities in a 'new' country. Australian culture then must have seemed 'unformed' in the very things that mattered most, in abstraction, design, and technologies of production. Writing about emigré weavers — Solvig Baas Becking, Erika Gretschel (now Semmler), Elisabeth Nagle, Jutta Feddersen, Ann Berney and Marcella Hempel — Diana Wood Conroy (herself a tapestry weaver and an influential writer on textiles) observes that they 'had a profound belief in weaving processes as part of human civilisation'. [4]   Through the structure of weaves and repetitive process, these weavers could 'extend the sense of structural order to the multiple ordering systems found in the natural world' and in doing so, rebuild shattered civilisations and construct a place for themselves in a 'young', raw country.

The modernist philosophies and professional attitudes of this generation of artist/designers were decisive in laying the foundations of the national crafts infrastructure and securing a footing in the public funding of the arts through the newly formed Australia Council (formed as the Australian Council for the Arts in 1973). At the infrastructural level as well as in critical debate in these years, a compelling discourse emerged which served to distinguish crafts practice from art, while legitimating the crafts in their struggle for recognition by arts funding bodies, teaching institutions and the museum-gallery system. The crafts community was consolidated across potentially divisive differences in media, techniques, and traditions, bridging the gap between production crafts and studio crafts.

The evolution of contemporary crafts within the national arts infrastructure has deeply influenced the character and recognition of Australian textiles practice. Current policy and funding of contemporary craft organisations and initiatives has its roots in the 1973 formation of separate Crafts and Visual Arts Boards of the Australia Council, their subsequent

Elena Gallegos
Entrevidas (1994)
woven cotton, galvanised wire
61 x 53 x 22 cm

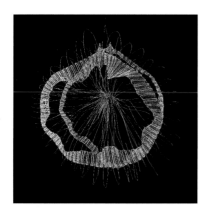

amalgamation to form the Visual Arts/Craft Board (now Fund) in 1987, and a belated realisation in the early 1990s that the once-comparable funding of visual art and craft was becoming increasingly inequitable. As a result, the Australia Council has been proactive in supporting the crafts, particularly through its nurturing of critical writing and innovative curatorial practice, attracting distinguished writers and curators from a wide disciplinary range to contribute to the crafts. So, for the present at least, Australian practitioners, writers and curators do not eschew the term 'craft', eliding it into 'art' and/or 'design'. By the same token, they avoid valorising craft into a coherent, unified practice, preferring to explore its multi-dimensional histories, contexts and practices.

Talking to colleagues from different countries, one becomes aware of how deeply these issues related to infrastructure, histories and perceptions of national cultures shape the career options and creative avenues open to practitioners and the recognition their work attracts. Reviewing Peter Dormer's *The Culture of Craft* [5] recently, I began to reconsider his 'conservatism' in the light of the deep artisanal traditions that underlie British craft. In the Australian context, those traditions were ruptured by convict and colonial immigration. In the exhilarating heyday of the studio crafts movement of the 1970s, it seemed as if there had been no earlier formative Australian craft traditions. In the quintessential modernism of the studio crafts movement, this perceived absence endowed a myth of Antipodean originality while simultaneously nurturing an internationalist eclecticism, characterised by a sense of commonality with British and American practitioners, a deep respect for Japanese traditions, and an unwitting but valorising primitivism in relation to textile traditions of 'third world' nations and indigenous cultures, from which techniques and images were readily appropriated.

The lines connecting Australia and the United Kingdom have been broken and re-forged many times over two centuries. By the 1970s, many key textile artists including Valerie Kirk and Patrick Snelling had been born in the UK. Others had undertaken some of their professional education there. Archie Brennan, in particular, contributed to the development of Australian tapestry: Kay Lawrence is one of a number of significant artists who trained in Edinburgh and has, in turn, influenced many others through her practice, her teaching and her community-based public art projects, of which the Parliament House embroideries (1984-6) are the best known. Others turned to the United States for their training and sustenance: for example Liz Jeneid spent time in the Black Mountains, North Carolina. Informed by travel, on-going research and sustained practice, many artists now working within the university system have reinforced values of conceptual clarity and interdisciplinary cross-fertilisation. Formal systems of education were supplemented by journals and magazines such as *Textile Fibre Forum* (initially *Fibre Forum*) edited by Janet de Boer since 1981 and *Object*, a major national craft journal published by the Centre for Contemporary Craft in Sydney.

As a consequence, textile art here has deep roots in the British and American traditions. Just as the histories of non-indigenous Australian settlement intersects with the histories of other nations, so the formation of Australian textiles seemed to be one of post-colonial grafts on 'parent' root-stocks. In fact, these grafts contributed to two centuries of Australian textile practice, which has incorporated professional hand–production and design for manufacture as well as domestic–produced decorative arts and objects of everyday and ritual use. Currently, a strength in Australian craft is a shared sense of the integration — and integrity — of creative work in which exhibition, production work and design are seen to be mutually

Ruth Hadlow
Travel Wagga (1997-98)
leaves, thread
approx. 200 x 90 cm

Valerie Kirk
Looking Back (1997)
tapestry and embroidery, wool and cotton
20 x 20 cm

enhancing. For example, Melbourne-based textile designers, Andrea McNamara and Patrick Snelling, have integrated exhibition work with limited-run production and fabric design — as well as publishing a successful textbook on printed textiles and innovating at the interface of textiles and computer technologies. [6] Distinguished by virtuoso weaving and rich use of colour, Liz Williamson's scarves and wraps have acquired national cult status. Australian fashion is enlivened by the contributions of artist-designer-makers, a number of whom have founded designer labels and significant production companies. Pam Gaunt's work asks elegant questions of the fashion industry, while the dramatic wearable garments of Patricia Black, on the cusp of art and fashion, are highly prized in Italy.

It was a corollary of the consolidation and professionalisation of the studio crafts movement that an insistent distinction was drawn between professional or 'serious' crafts and the increasingly popular domestic and hobby crafts. This distinction was reinforced by public funding of the arts from the 1970s to the early 1990s. But, concurrently, a number of textile artists were strongly influenced by the counter-cultural values and 'country' lifestyles of the 1970s and second-wave feminism of the 1970s and 1980s. The valorisation of women's domestic craft traditions ran counter to the notion of 'excellence' in the crafts and public funding bodies, but feminism offered a basis for identifying with domestic traditions and cut right across the art/craft boundaries that were being reinforced elsewhere. In 1979, for example, a group of Sydney artists formed the Women's Domestic Needlework Group to present an exhibition of women's domestic needlework, titled *The D'Oyley Show*, with the aim of re-valuing the 'hidden' traditions of fancywork. And many artists worked with textiles and detritus of the home to make artworks which explored aspects of women's lives.

Concurrently, Australian decorative arts history was becoming increasingly accessible through exhibitions and related publications highlighting the collections of major national and state art galleries. The history of 'making' in post-settlement Australia has been brought to light by historians and curators — one thinks of the work of Grace Cochrane, Judith O'Calloghan, Kylie Winkworth, Noris Ioannou, Margaret Rolfe, Glenda King, Jennifer Lamb, Michael Rolfe, John McPhee, Michael Bogle, Robert Bell, Jim Logan, Geoffrey Edwards, Margie West and Christopher Menz, amongst many others. With the impetus of the Australian Bicentenary in 1988 came celebrations, investigations and contestations of Australian cultural history in which distinctions between professional and amateur, and public and domestic, seemed anachronistic. Significant among publications which retrieve Australian textile history are Jennifer Isaacs' *The Gentle Arts: 200 Years of Australian Women's Domestic and Decorative Arts* (1987), Grace Cochrane's *The Crafts Movement in Australia: A History* (1992) and *Heritage: The National Women's Art Book* (1995), edited by Joan Kerr. [7]

A strong interest across disciplines and artforms in narrative, memory, identity and performance, which has spanned the 1980s and 1990s, has been a creative touchstone for many textile artists. Artists now explore personal, family and community lives through their work and the stories they attach to them. Complementing the histories of professional crafts practice, those stories re-map Australian textiles, criss-crossing domestic and professional practices as frequently as they cross the oceans to their countries of origin and reach back through generations for a sense of historical depth. This sense of lineage informs the work of Jan Irvine-Nealie: *Virtue of Obsession* (1994), an exhibition which she curated, explored her own textiles matrilineage, and honoured the domestic work of her mother, grandmother and great-grandmother. At last, the idea of the 'decorative arts' can shake its stigma of 'trivial' and museum collections enable makers, curators and writers to trace Australian antecedents to contemporary practice.

Similarly, the customs and labour of everyday life and 'vernacular objects' need not be invested with nostalgia or condescension. As Jim Logan commented in his introduction to the National Gallery of Australia's 1998 exhibition, *Everyday Art: Australian Folk Art*, the 'wilfully nationalistic vernacular language in the decorative arts answered the needs of a culture on the cusp of Federation'. [8] The 'make-do' improvisations of times of scarcity — from the 'waggas' made with material from corn, flour and wheat sacks, to the quilts made in Changi prisoner-of-war camp — retain emotional residues. Improvisation in the face of hardship is deeply integrated in narratives of survival which figure largely in constructs of nationhood in Australia.

Australian textile artists today constitute a culturally diverse community. Contemporary practice has been enriched by migration, not only from the UK, USA and Europe, but also from Latin America, from the Middle East and from the Asia-Pacific region. Narrative histories — whether articulated as personal or collective — have been the groundswell of a range of postcolonial perspectives. Artists exploring non-Western cultural connections and diasporic experience are imparting energy and diversity to contemporary textiles at present. The recent work of Elena Gallegos, Keiko Amenomori Schmeisser, Greg Leong, Nelia Justo and Hanh Nguyet Ngo — to take just six examples — explores the fractured, constructed identities of multi-cultural experience.

Australians have positioned themselves in the histories of professional and artisanal crafts, as well as in domestic, family and community narratives, without necessarily figuring these as unbroken chains. They have turned for inspiration and a sense of belonging, not only to Britain, Europe and the United States but also — and increasingly — to the Asia-Pacific region. At the same time, many Indigenous and non-indigenous artists share a deeply held commitment to the 'reconciliation process' that might yet enable all Australians to love the country and honour those who have cared for it over thousands of years. Many textile artists, such as Ruth Hadlow and Tori de Mestre, not only give expression to their own deep attachment to the land, but also pay their respects to Indigenous artists and cultures. Elsje van Keppel's beautiful patterned, layered, pieced and stitched wall pieces draw subtle analogies between the natural world and its processes of erosion and transformation and those of the body, self and spirit.

Our textiles and fibre art have roots in Australian history and they are embedded in a distinctive Australian understanding of the nature and context of craft. The work featured in this book by Gloria Petyarre, Jeannie Petyarre, Ada Bird Petyarre, Nora Petyarre, Old Polly Gnale, Amy Napangardi and Lena Pwerle (members of the Utopia Awely Batik Aboriginal Corporation), Patricia Black, Elena Gallegos, Pam Gaunt, Ruth Hadlow, Jan Irvine Nealie, Elsje van Keppel (King), Valerie Kirk, Tori de Mestre and Patrick Snelling graphically demonstrates the breadth of practice and the diversity of cultural and artistic lineages that make up Australian textile art.

Professor Sue Rowley
Chair of Contemporary Australian Art History,
University of New South Wales College of Fine Arts,
President of the Centre for Contemporary Craft

Tori de Mestre
Mungeribar
river stone, cotton thread,
guinea-fowl feathers
35 cm wide

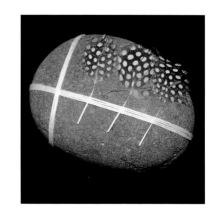

Artists

Awely is really important. It is Aityerr, the Dreamtime, when the world was created. Awely dance and song makes people happy and strong when they are sick. Awely holds up country. Women have the Awely; not men. Awely is everything. Awely is the whole lot.

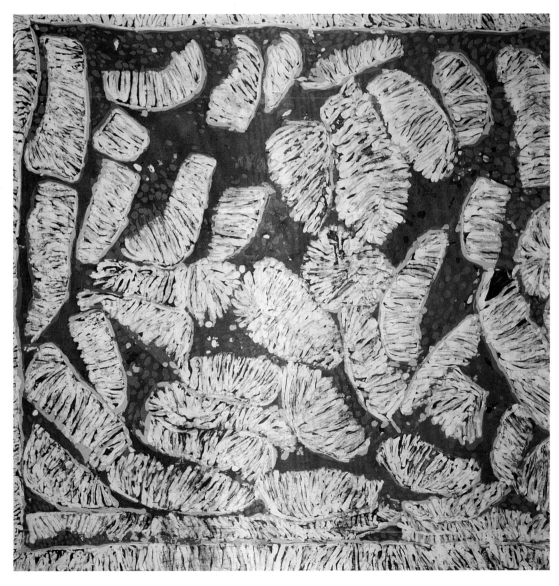

left:
Nora Petyarre
Honey Ant Dreaming (detail)
silk, batik

above:
Old Polly Gnale
Bush Grass 'Ntange (detail)
silk, batik

Utopia Awely Batik Aboriginal Corporation

Amy Napangardi
untitled (1996)
silk satin, batik
1.2 x 3 m

Utopia

18 October 1998
Utopia Cultural Centre & Utopia Awely Batik Aboriginal Corporation
PNMB 200 Utopia via Alice Springs
Northern Territory 0872

Dear Mr Koumis,

Our organisation welcomes your enquiry concerning sales of our paintings compared to sales of our batiks.

Gloria Petyarre is a good indicator – one of her best quality paintings the size of a silk –, i.e. 120 x 300 cm, would conservatively fetch about $6,000 – $8,000 on the gallery wall. An equivalent batik silk, taking six times as much time and effort to make (not to mention the necessary training and technical skill required) would fetch only about $1,500 – $2,000 at the most. Emily Kngwarre's batiks are currently auctioning at about $15,000 compared to an average $30,000 for a small painting.

The instincts of our artists are to be natural mark-makers delineating a story with spiritual significance. Whatever medium the indigenous artist chooses to work in, whether coloured sand with the finger, wax and dye painted with a brush onto silk, paint brushed onto canvas, paint or natural pigments as body painting using splayed twigs and the ubiquitous finger: the power imbued in the marks, and the ceremonial import of the work, remains the same.

Yet the modern art market has set artificial notions of 'value' construed out of the history of European art, tempered by good ol' yankee capitalism and centuries of ingrained gender prejudice against women's work. All this rates textiles a poor cousin to painting. However, our Corporation quietly shows paintings beside batiks just to jolt old notions and the fine art connoisseurs usually succumb to the sensuousness of the silks! They are confronted with the juxtaposition of static canvases in flat matte, and the immediacy of tactile, rippling liquid colour!

Hope this is of interest.

With best wishes,

Jan Ross-Manley
Art Co-ordinator
Utopia Awely Batik Aboriginal Corporation

Lena Pwerle
Lizard Dreaming
silk satin, batik
1.2 x 3 m

This is Alhaltere and Atnankere Dreaming for country. This is 'Little Lizard', 'Thorny Devil Lizard', 'Emu', 'Dog', 'Long Thin Yam' and 'Yam Flower Dreaming'. Also 'Angerema Dreaming' (dogwood tree seeds), that's the bean tree. Awely is really important. It is Aityerr, The Dreamtime when everything began. Awely dance and song makes people happy and strong when they are sick. With Awely they get fat again. Awely holds up country. Women have the Awely; not men. The body painting is Awely. We use special music sticks when we dance and sing; not the usual clap sticks. Our Awely goes a long way from Utopia right up to Tennant Creek and all the way to Three Ways where it branches off somewheres. Might be Arnhem Land. At Three Ways is 'Achingarakurra', a sacred waterhole. The people from long time back have been knowing it as a dangerous place. They will only drink the water if they first put leaves in the waterhole. The leaves make it alright. The body scars (cicatrices) are made to heal sickness and they are Awely also. Awely is everything. Awely is the whole lot. Our Awely is from my grandfather and grandmother on my father's side and my father. That's it. Kathleen Kemarre has been teaching me for a long time since I was a kid. I never lose it. I pass it on to my nieces and cousins. My granddaughter she knows.

Gloria Tamerre Petyarre

Gloria Tamerre Petyarre
Awely Body Painting 1997
wax and acrylic on silk, 500 x 120cm

Selected Exhibitions for the Batik Artists Collective

1981   *Floating Forests of Silk*, Adelaide Festival Centre, SA

1983   *Utopia Batik,* Crafts Council of the Northern Territory, Alice Springs

1984   *Utopia Batik Araluen Art Centre*, Alice Springs, NT

1986   *Utopia Batik,* Crafts Council of Australia, Canberra

1987   *Utopia Batik,* Freemantle Arts Centre, WA

1989   *Aboriginal Art from Utopia*, Gallery Gabrielle Pizzi Melbourne, Vic

           Utopian Art, Austral Gallery, St Louis, Missouri, USA

1990   *A Picture Story*, Tandanya

           Ten Women Artists, Macquarie Galleries, Sydney

1991   *Aboriginal Art and Spirituality,* High Court of Australia, Canberra, ACT

1995   *Hot Wax/Utopia Silks*, Westpac Gallery, Victorian Arts Centre, Melbourne

1996   *Native Titled Now*, Tandanya National Cultural Institute, Adelaide, SA

1997-98 *Utopia/The Paris Silks Collection*, Parc de la Villette, Paris, France

1998   *Utopia Prints & Batiks*, Hogarth Galleries, Sydney, New South Wales

           Origins and New Perspectives/Contemporary Australian Textiles, Centre for Art Promotion

           to coincide with *9th International Triennale of Tapestry,* Lodz, Poland

           Utopia/New Work, Framed Gallery, Darwin

           Hand to Cloth, Metro Craft Centre, Melbourne, Vic

           Mapping Identity, Centre for Contemporary Craft, Sydney NSW (tour)

1999   *Aboriginal Textiles in Fashion Exhibition*, Gallery Gabriel, Pizzi, Melbourne Fashion Festival

           Textiles Exhibition, Sturt Gallery, Mittagong NSW

above:

Ada Bird Petyarre

at Parc de la Villette, Paris

Selected Awards

Premier award, Metro Craft Centre, *Hand to Cloth Exhibition*, Melbourne

(to Rosemary Petyarre/Utopia)

Selected Collections

Araluen Art Centre, Alice Springs, NT

Robert Holmes a Court Collection

Museum and Art Gallery of the NT

Powerhouse Museum, Sydney, NSW

Art Gallery of South Australia, Adelaide

Queensland Art Gallery, Brisbane

Museum of Victoria, Melbourne

National Gallery of Australia, Canberra

National Gallery of Victoria, Melbourne

Queen Victoria Museum and Art Gallery, Launceston, Tasmania

Museum of African and Oceanic Arts, Paris, France

web site

www.utopiaculture.org.au

Utopia

The processes I use are often metaphors for nature's processes, ones which naturally weather and create a surface. This object is not specifically about the landscape, or about the desert, or about Niagara. But it was stimulated by the experience of being in a particular place at a particular time. It is about an almost indescribable feeling of fragility and even vulnerability.

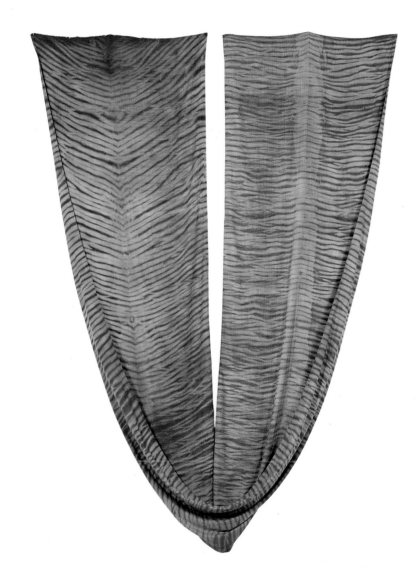

right:
animal vegetable (1996)
handspun and woven silk, resist dyed,
vegetable dyed
496 x 87 cm

left:
parched, Niagara (1994)
natural dyes on paper, framed
145 x 79 x 4 cm

Elsje van Keppel

In 1989 I returned to Amsterdam, taking my first international exhibition to my original homeland. Like many Australians who had arrived as children, I had been experiencing a sense of displacement. I was looking for a sense of connectedness, and felt the need to identify with the long traditions of European culture.

Soon after I came back, I went out into the bush on a trip to Ethel River, in Western Australia. It was here, walking along the side of the riverbed and cliffs of beautifully tessellated rocks, that I felt the spirituality and energy so reminiscent of a cathedral. This was where I began to understand that the vastness of time I had been searching for in the culture of Europe was, in fact, part of the continuity of the natural world. The land itself has provided the counterbalance to a perceived lack of historical depth for white Australians. I realised that the bush and desert of the interior have played a central role in the development of our national cultural imagination.

So in *Cathedral Floor — Ethel River*, the layering and shifting fabric is reminiscent of the layering of the rock-wall I found there. The processes involved in making this piece, the dyeing, layering and stitching, become both the subject of the work and metaphor for the processes of the natural world. I hope the viewer can see in the fragility and transparency of the pieces the precarious nature of the relationship between the natural world and those who inhabit it. This work also has references to the Australian landscape tradition and to the Impressionists. Using bush leaves and bark, the fabric was dyed by the river. In the technique of resist-dyeing, some areas of cloth are left untouched, showing their original state. I see this process as one which creates history – a history brought about not only by the passage of time and by natural cycles of growth and decay, but also by the changes resulting from human intervention. That history is reiterated through the rhythm and marks of the stitches, which speak of the desert, the soil, nature.

Dust to Dust speaks both of our compulsion to build and of nature as an unfolding process. Meaning is intrinsic to making; my works have developed by abstracting the natural course of things. The underlying structure comes from the log cabin quilt. Since the 17th century, this pattern has been an icon of home, hearth and a safe return. The system of fabric strips, originating from the image of logs placed one on top of another, is a metaphor for women's practicality, resourcefulness and frugality.

regeneration (1995)
hand-stitched silk fabric, silk thread,
vegetable dye, batik
200 x 160 cm

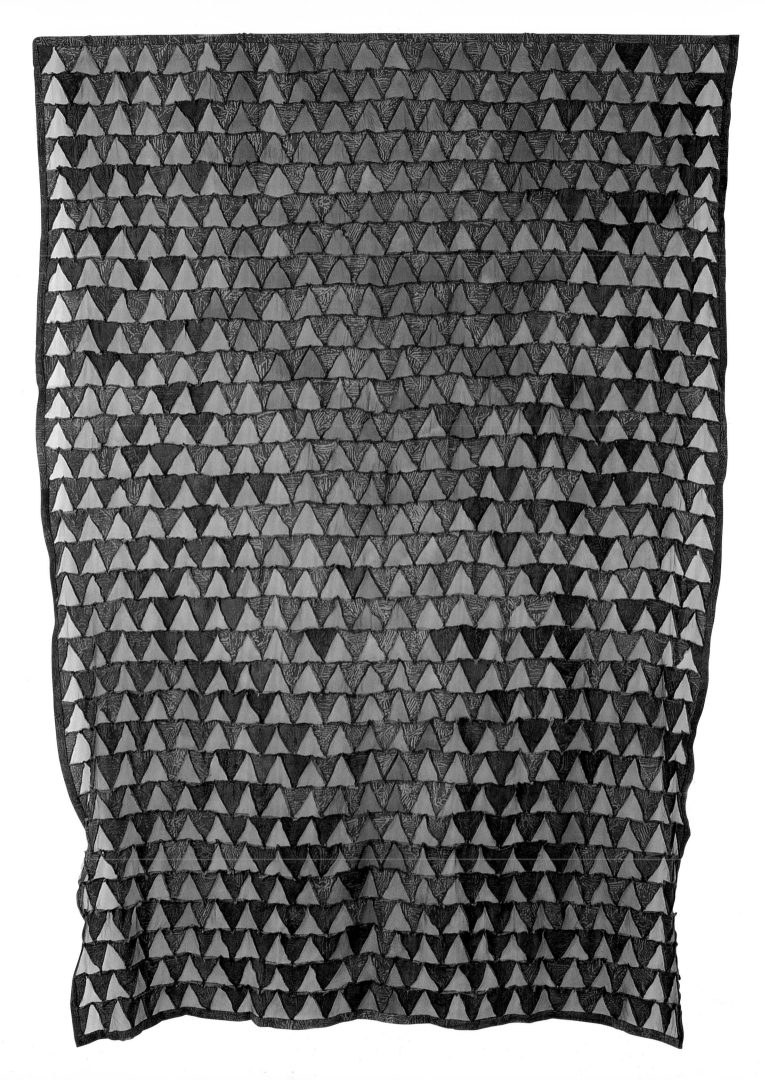

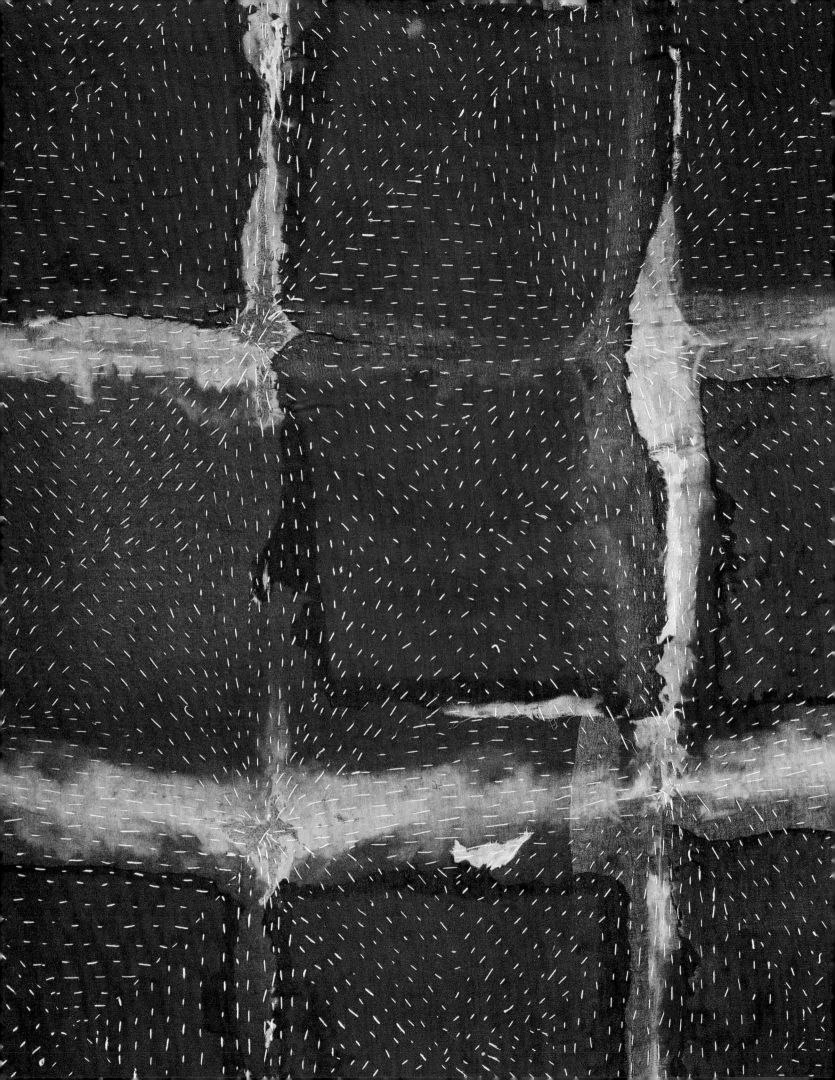

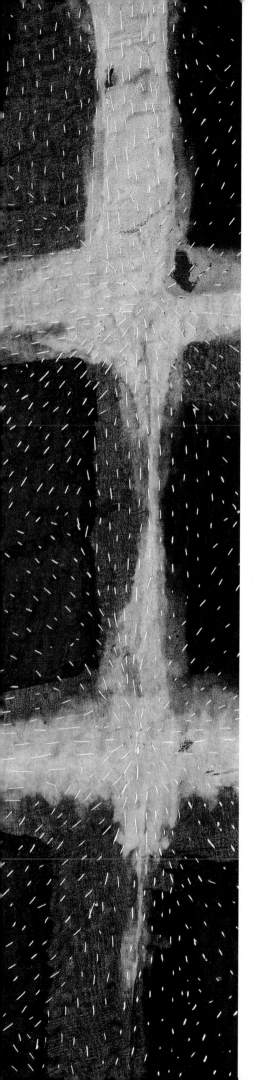

dark night (1997) (detail)
silk and wool fabrics, silk thread, indigo and discharge-dyed
150 x 102 cm

My work often evolves very slowly. I usually have a number of things on the go, half-cooked. It's been five years since my first interaction with this fabric. Stitching is a real treat, a retreat to a private place. The quiet pleasure it gives is not just from the physical enjoyment of sewing a firm, pliable fabric. It's also about creating order, making something whole again, watching a new pattern emerge.

The batik images, printed by friends in Indonesia, have evolved from marks I stumbled across once in a building near to my home which was undergoing renovation. The red dust of the bricks was exposed by scars in the walls, lacerations through layer upon layer of pastel paint.

Just as the marks and colours of the base fabrics are products of chance and improvisation, so too the construction of the log cabin quilt is open to the distortions of the making process. Too rigid a plan kills the energy; the rhythmic tracery of the making must be free to breathe, otherwise materials will conform obediently but lifelessly to a pattern.

The weaknesses of the finished textile – the ripples, tears, patches, frayed edges, selvedges and threads, are all important elements of the integrated piece.

Although there are references to my Dutch heritage, for example with form and structure, I believe my work acknowledges both Australian and European culture. An engagement with the natural world has allowed me to establish a critical distance between myself and the world of art history. There are those who appear to seek to dominate the land and its resources: the modernist approach to nature is through control and reduction. However, I hope to represent a relationship with the natural world based on a mutuality of process, in which 'history' is one element of natural processes rather than its over-writing.

Elsje van Keppel

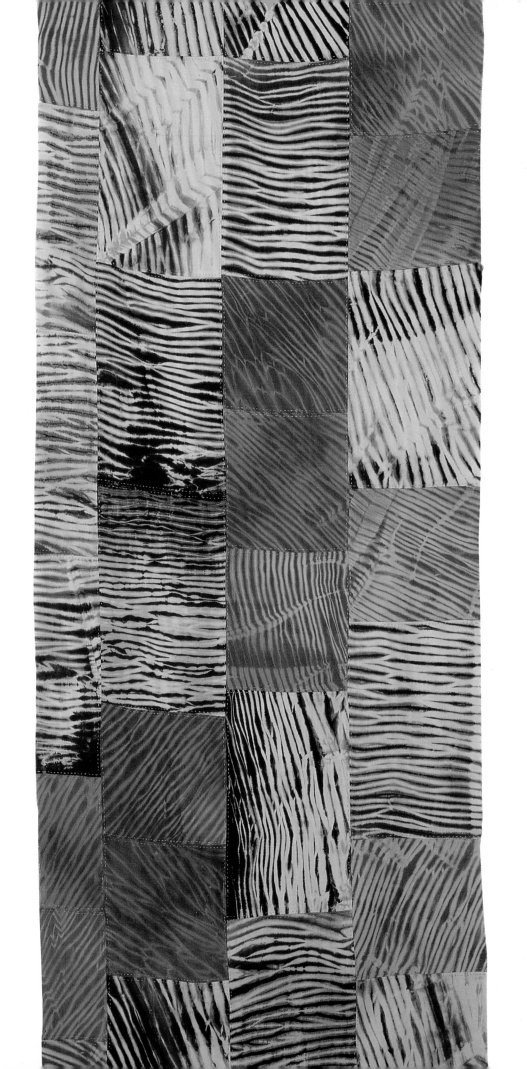

in the making (1996)
wool fabric, linen thread,
resist-dyed,
vegetable-dyed,
hand-stitched
335 x 103 cm

Cloth is much more than a two-dimensional surface. Each different fabric has its own qualities, its own characteristic way of moving, its own fluidity made by the fibre it is made of, its own particular structure. This fabric (left) is made of locally grown Merino fibre, very tightly spun and woven. It will take a lot of resistance and a lot of dyestuff.

Born
1947 The Netherlands
1952 came to Australia

Education and Awards

1972	Curtin University of Technology, WA
1978	Goldsmiths' College, University of London
1989	Grant, Department for the Arts, WA
1991	Grant, Visual Arts and Crafts Fund, Australia Council
1997-98	Creative Fellowship, Visual Arts and Crafts Fund, Australia Council

Selected Exhibitions

1976	Old Fire Station, Perth, WA (solo)
1980	Miller Gallery, Perth, WA (solo)
1982	*Craftworks by Twelve Western Australians,* Art Gallery of Western Australia, Perth, WA
1983	*Paperworks,* Art Gallery of Western Australia, Perth, WA
1989	Stov, Amsterdam, The Netherlands (solo)
	International Arts Triennial, Art Gallery of Western Australia, Perth, WA
1990	Meat Market Centre, Melbourne (solo)
1991-93	*Threads of Journeys,* DFAT Canberra, (international tour)
1994	University of Tasmania (Tasmanian tour) (solo)
1995	*The Art of the Object* (S American tour)
	The 8th International Triennale of Tapestry, Lodz, Poland
1995-97	*Crossing Borders,* University of Wollongong (USA tour)
1997-99	Craftwest Gallery, Perth (national tour) (solo)
1998	*Contemporary Australian Textiles,* Lodz, Poland
	Third International Craft Triennial, Art Gallery of Western Australia, Perth, WA

Collections

Ararat Regional Gallery, Victoria
Art Gallery of Western Australia, Perth, WA
Edith Cowan University, WA
Museum and Art Gallery of the Northern Territory, Darwin
Parliament House, Canberra
The Powerhouse Museum, Sydney
Queensland Art Gallery, Brisbane
Tamworth National Fibre Collection, NSW
Victorian State Craft Collection, Melbourne

Elsje van Keppel

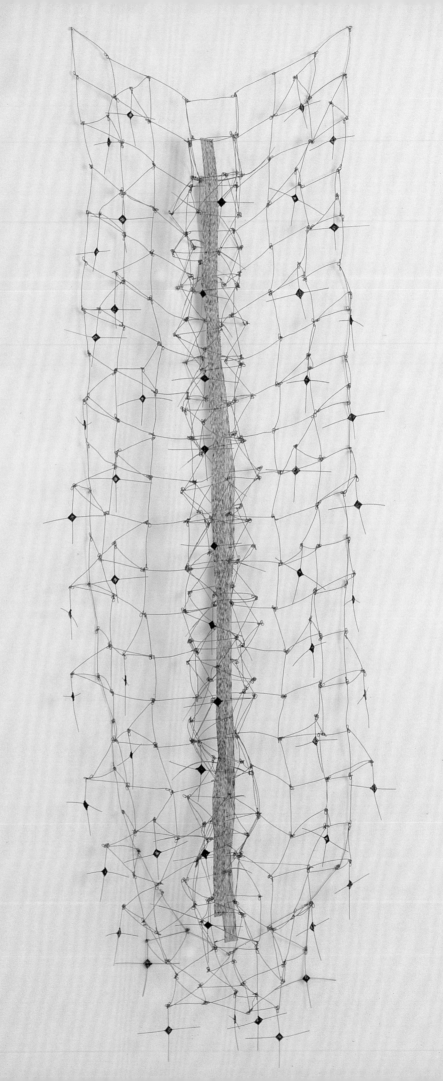

30

right:
Entrevidas (1994)
woven cotton, galvanised wire
61 x 53 x 22 cm

As an emigré, a major theme in my work is the jagged sense of loss and insecurity resulting from exile. My work symbolises my proof-of-place-in-the-world, although without an exact locale.

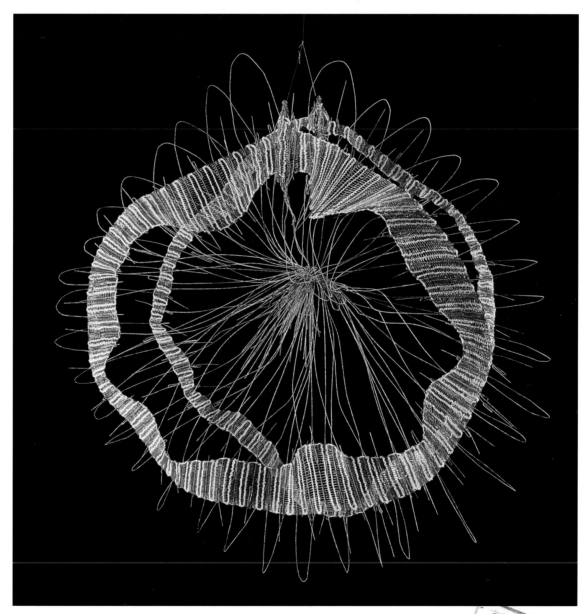

left:
Political Fragility (1991)
woven silk, galvanised wire
150 x 50 cm

Elena Gallegos

Untitled (1987)
silk, wire, electrical components
52 x 47 cm

This piece (right) incorporates electronic connectors. I do not understand them, but they are beautiful. A friend who knows electronics later explained to me that the way the connectors are actually woven means there would be no passing of energy, no communication. So my weaving, unconsciously, had realised my intentions.

The piece is a mirror of technology. Media is quite inaccessible, as I see it, it is not in the service of the community. But I love the look of it, how intricate the wires are. It is like watching television – you may not understand how it works but it is fun to gaze at! Technology comes from an alien world.

Time is money, so contemporary society would have us believe. Consumerism and ambition are today's buzz words. I look on weaving as my act of defiance. Drawn into this time-consuming and uneconomical activity, I am drawn beyond, into a sense of cosmic timelessness. Here, priorities are reshaped, hierarchies transformed.

I became involved in textiles because of their vital presence in the lives of human beings, both anthropologically and metaphorically. Entwined is the material and its treatment, creating the possibility of an entirely fresh poetic association.

Structural principles determine form, yet the physical is only there to articulate the gap between the spaces we inhabit in the realms of spirit and matter. I see it as a kind of fissure through which I look out into the unknown. The transience of material life is something that I enjoy observing. Some of my works are deliberately left to decay in the elements.

I have a lot of pleasure in being alive, and in the joy of working every day. Recently I've been working with feathers. Primarily every movement is the outcome of my thinking process: in real terms I'm putting in another weft, inserting a feather or a metal piece – I know what each one means to me.

Political fragility (page 30)
This weaving is like a cloak or a mantle reaching the point of disappearance. In some way it represents my own body in a transparent structure. The tiny black dots are the only clearly visible feature. They are like the devil's eye, a symbol you find in Mexico for example. It is a mantle of evil eyes, so that when people look at you they cannot put anything bad on you, no evil thought will harm you. It is not a physical thing, it is a spiritual cloak, a transparent armature.

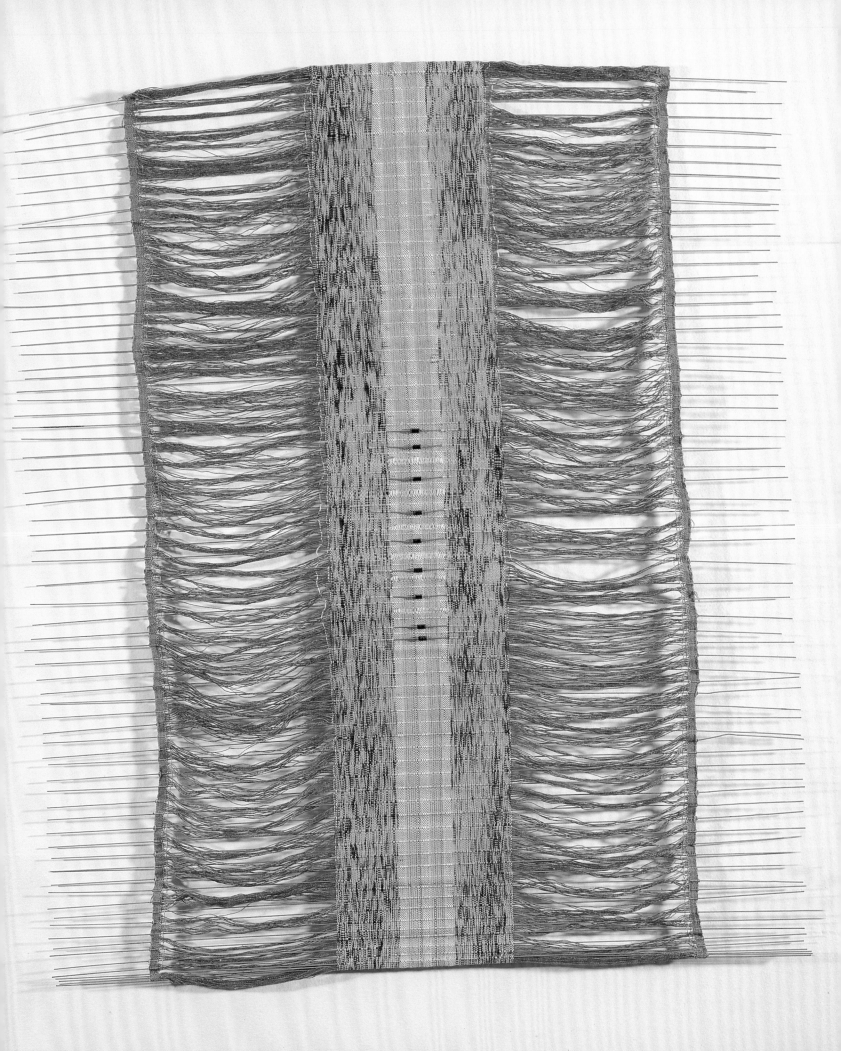

I was at my kitchen sink. Suddenly I saw a little lizard. I thought I would pull it out of the sink, but the tail came out jumping at me. I felt so heavy-handed, and guilty too! I did not realise until someone told me later that lizards actually shed their tail as a way of defending themselves. I felt very relieved! A decoy, you leave your body behind, something to stand in for you while the real you disappears.

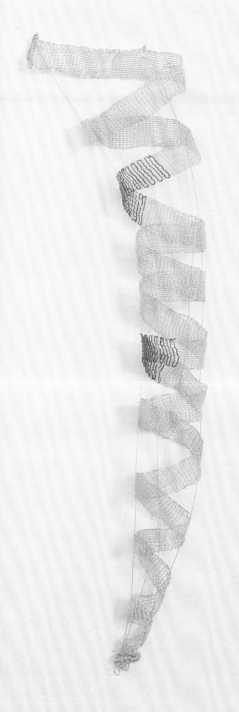
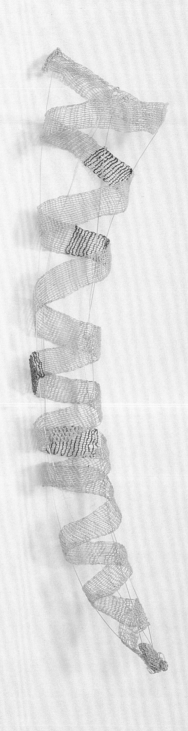

Tails (1993)
woven copper, cotton
60 x 15 cm

Elena Gallegos

I started to pack rolls of newspaper as a way of exorcising memories of a time when newspapers suddenly disappeared from circulation in Chile, truth never to be known.

I have something to say as transparent
                              and incomprehensible
As birdsong in wartime.

Here, in a corner where I sat down
To smoke my first cigarette of freedom
Uncomfortable in happiness, trembling
In case I break a flower, hurt some bird
…
Much is not wanted by the world. One thing
Minimal.
Like bad steering just before the accident

But
Exactly
In
The opposite direction

We've worshipped danger enough and it's time
                              we were paid back.

I dream of an uprising in the realms of evil, and of war
like that which Matisse waged on chiaruscuro
and colour shading.

from *Villa Natacha*, by Odysseas Elytis

Roll up (1981)
paper, cotton,
beaded installation
21 x 21 cm

Entrevidas (page 31)

The two woven circles move a little bit, so you do not know which one is going to be in front of the other, there is a kinetic aspect. They symbolise water holes, which are essential to indigenous culture. There is not a lot of water in the centre of Australia, they are vital for survival. But there are fewer and fewer of them, and right now, some say, they are being made deliberately unusable by current agrarian practices. Dirtying your own water hole? The circle is there and yet not quite there. The use or abuse of our resources, the possibility of disappearance, of dying out...

Born   1952 Santiago, Chile
              1974 came to Australia

Education and Awards
1982-85   BA Visual Art, Canberra School of Art
1988   Visual Arts and Craft Board, Australia Council Grant

Selected Exhibitions
1991   *Political Fragility*, Galerie Constantinople, Queanbeyan NSW (solo)
1993   *Discerning Textiles*, Goulburn Regional Art Gallery (solo)
           Recent Work, Australian Girls Own Gallery (aGOG) Canberra (solo)
1994   *Entrevidas*, Lismore Regional Gallery (solo)
           Crossing Borders, Contemporary Australian Textile Art (USA tour)
1995   *Traces of Textiles*, Craft ACT Gallery
1996   *12th Tamworth Fiber Textile Biennial,* Tamworth NSW
           Second Look, Prospect Textile Biennial, Adelaide
1997   *Bold Bags and Old Baggage*, Hobart, Tasmania

Art/Works and Projects
1989-90   Citizenship Banner Project, National Campaign on Citizenship, Wollongong City Council
           Multicultural Textile Project, Wollongong City Council
1991   *Silk on the Shore Installation,* World Environment Day, Artist-in-Residence, Bellrive Community Centre
           Shining Thread, Community Art Project, City of Clarence Municipal Chambers, Tasmania
1992   *West Coast Woman,* Community Art Project of Australia (Tasmanian Division) inc.
1993   Artist-in-Residence, Brisbane Ethnic Music and Arts Centre
           Gung Ho to Paradise, Community Theatre Project, Trades and Labour Council of Queensland
1996   *Rivers Silk*, Community Art Project, Tasmanian Council
1997   *Children's Week*, Banner Project, sponsored by Canberra Cultural Centre

Collections
           Australian National Gallery

Elena Gallegos

My landscapes are a dramatic stage for presenting ideas, often reflecting some philosophical or social issue. In *All Australian*, I am considering the consequences of our cultural mix in this one continent. What are our social issues and what direction will come of this? How will we be swept toward our future values?

left:
Bringing on the Rain (1997)
airbrush dyed silk, wool fill
hand-stitched
62 x 145 cm

above:
All Australian (1994)
airbrush dyed silk, wool fill
hand-stitched
110 x 170 cm

Jan Irvine-Nealie

The land is my abiding inspiration. Having grown up in the country and having spent years in isolated and desert areas, I feel the Aboriginal sense of 'earth as mother'. Even during my years of city living, I have been able to draw personal well-being from relating to the spirit of the land and how it feels.

Before humankind there was terra firma, which exists with or without our issues. In spite of human interference, land still exudes energies to nurture and influence the life it sustains. My landscapes are a dramatic stage for presenting ideas, often reflecting some philosophical or social issue.

While developing my original idea, I reflect my world as I see it and, in this sense, my work is contemporary. But it is the second process, the stitching, which satisfies and links me back into the chain of the human condition. My process of stitching through padded layers firmly locates me within a needlework tradition. This stitching is a direct link to the needlework traditions of my own family. My great-grandmother, my grandmother and mother were all involved in some sort of textile activity. They have been a significant influence on me and I am delighted to be part of that on-going tradition.

The patient and persistent drawing through of needle and thread has been the means of soothing the souls of my previous generations. I find stitching a meditative task which focuses me on the fuller meaning of the intuitive image I have created.

I applied my art training as a teacher, and spent my early career with Primary School children and later, to my great advantage, with tribal Aboriginal women in the Pitjantjatjara lands, in the north of South Australia. Employed as a sewing teacher, I had a 'waste not, want not' desire to make use of scraps of tie-dyed fabric on the workshop floor. When I wanted to make my spare time more creative I found myself making patchwork in the very traditional sort of way, but very quickly turned to my own designing, adapting my own interests and pursuing more delicate tonal rendition. So I went through various processes of piecing together tonal values in the 'found' fabrics, through overlaying sheer fabric chiffons and gauzes to get those tonal gradations that I was looking for, and then quite by chance found an airbrush that a potter friend of mine used to apply her glazes. With that I realised that I could apply dye in a way that gave me a great deal of subtlety and shifting of colour into colour.

The key elements in my design are landscape, light and movement.

First Sun (1995)
airbrush dyed silk, wool fill
hand-stitched
35 x 70 cm

Jan Irvine-Nealie

I deal with simple issues such as love of land and joy of spirit.

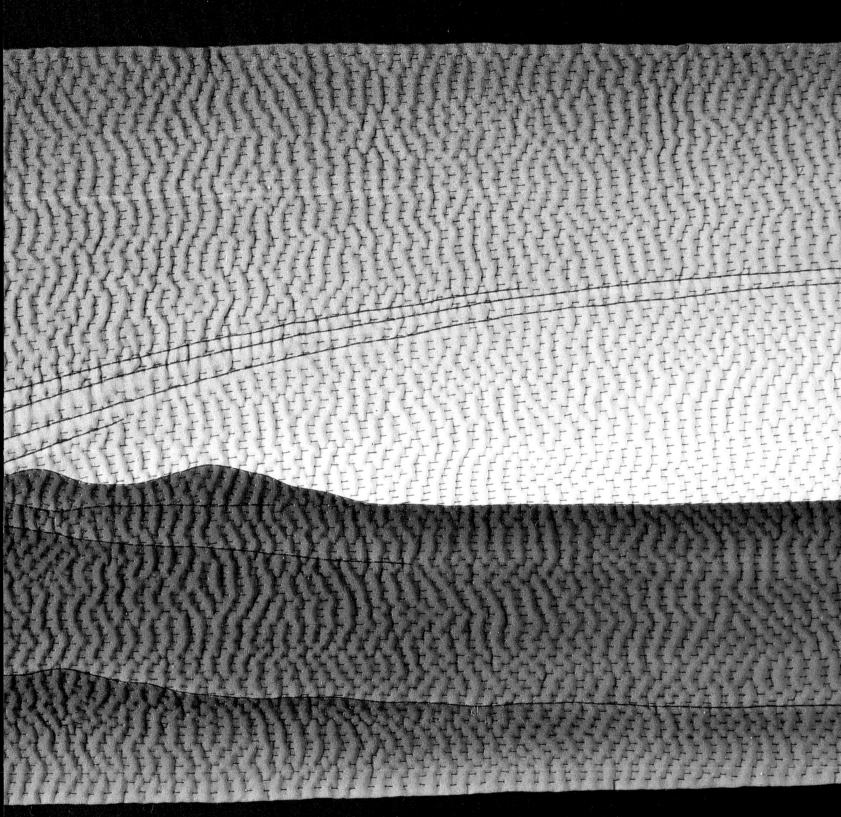

Signs of Promise Fulfilled (1998) (detail)
airbrush dyed silk, wool fill
hand-stitched
105 x 32 cm

Jan Irvine-Nealie

We draw back to ancient origins where our physical and ethereal selves join.

The image of each quilt is airbrushed with dye onto whole cloth. My dyed quilt top is always quilted, with sweeps and emphases designed to enhance the image. The gentle gathering effect of stitching creates a textured surface and gives greater depth and interest to the initial image.

Although I have trained in drawing and painting, I find a greater satisfaction in expressing my creative imagery in fabric. I enjoy the fall and flow of fabric, and its versatility.

Out of Gondwana (1995)
airbrush dyed silk, wool fill,
hand-stitched
90 x 145 cm

Born   1950, South Australia

Education and Awards

1968-70   SA School of Art, Adelaide, SA

1983-4   Adelaide Festival Centre Gallery, Adelaide, SA

1987   Artist-in-Residence, University of Wollongong School of Art, NSW

1988   *Quilt Australia '88*, Winner, political category

1996, 98   Artist-in-Residence, Queen Victoria Museum and Art Gallery, Launceston, Tasmania

Selected Exhibitions

1988   *Women '88 Awards*, Melbourne

            Quilt Australia '88, QGI, Sydney

1989   *Miniatures*, Crafts Council Gallery, Sydney, NSW (solo)

            Commission Textiles, Crafts Council Gallery, Sydney, NSW

            Quilt National, Ohio, USA (tour USA, Japan)

1991   Beaver Galleries, Canberra, ACT (solo)

            Threads of Journeys, DFAT – Canberra, ACT (international tour)

1993   *Discerning Textiles*, Goulburn Regional Gallery, NSW (Australian tour)

1994   *Virtue and Obsession*, Jam Factory Gallery SA (solo)

            Art of the Object, by Craft Australia (South American tour)

1995   *Australia Dreaming,* by Quilters' Guild Inc, for Darling Harbour, Sydney and Nagoya, Japan

            Running Stitch Wool Quilt Exhibition, National Wool Museum, Geelong, VIC

1996   *International Exchange Exhibition – Japan/Australia*, Nagoya, Japan

1995-97   *Crossing Borders*, by Wollongong University (USA tour)

1998   *The World Quilt '98 in Japan*, Nihon Vogue, Tokyo, Japan

2000   Queen Victoria Museum and Art Gallery, Launceston, Tasmania (solo)

Collections

            Queen Victoria Museum and Art Gallery, Launceston, Tasmania

            National Wool Museum, Geelong, VIC

            Powerhouse Museum, Sydney NSW

            Arrarat Regional Art Gallery, VIC

            Tamworth National Fibre Collection, Tamworth NSW

            Museum and Art Gallery of the Northern Territory, Darwin, NT

Publications

1993   *Decorative Arts & Design from the Powerhouse Museum*, Powerhouse, Sydney ISBN 1 86317 025 1, ISBN 1 86317 026 X

1994   *Contemporary Embroidery*, Anne Morrell, Merehurst, London ISBN 0 289 80105 2

1995   *Australia Dreaming – Quilts to Nagoyo,* Quilters Guild Inc, Fairfax Press, Sydney ISBN 1 86343 247 7

            88 Leaders of the Quilt World Today, Nihon, Vogue Japan NV 5227 ISBN 4 529 02557 8

web site   www.craftaus.com.au

Jan Irvine-Nealie

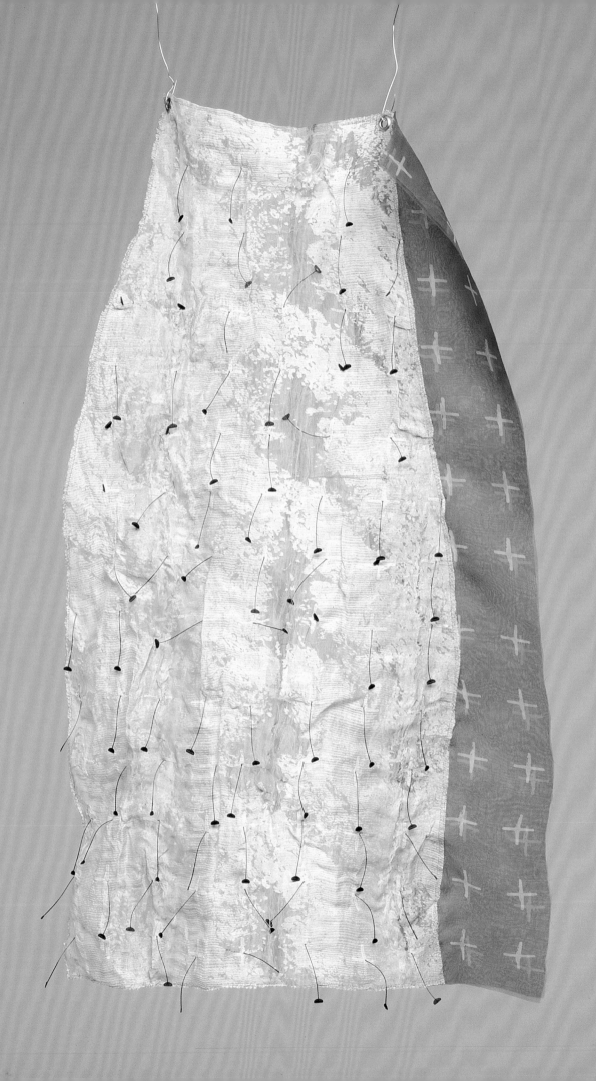

When you come to a Border – Cross It **is a visual metaphor for our own and other peoples' boundaries, as well as the challenge of combining the new and untried with a textile tradition.**

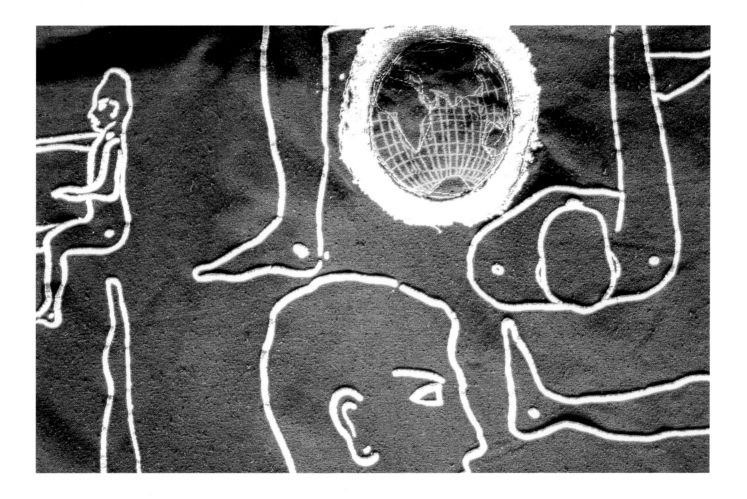

left:
When you come to a Border – Cross it (1998)
screen-printed silk, viscose & metal fabric,
pigmented inks and devoré, reactive and acid
dyes, metal eyelets, nylon tags, machine
stitched
93 x 48 cm

above:
Perfect People Print (detail) (1995)
machine stitched and appliqued cotton and linen cloth,
screen-printed pigmented and heat-sensitised inks,
acid-dyed silk, buttons
137 x 231 cm

Patrick Snelling

My brother and I grew up in London. As identical twins, we were referred to simply as 'the twins'. Our mother had us wearing name tags on our wrists, to make sure neither of us was fed twice. We were dressed as one. Our primary schoolteacher, the ironically named Miss Wardrobe, chalked the letters P and M on our foreheads at the beginning of each class so that she could tell us apart.

We separated ourselves consciously by whatever means: changing the colour of our shoelaces, walking home from school separately and in different directions, having separate groups of friends. The threatened loss of identity and the formation of a sense of singular self was a constant ordeal for us.

As a screen-printer and pattern-maker, I am constantly striving to develop and extend my technical competence, as well as to find new forms of visual expression.

Today textile philosophies concern lifestyle, personal expression and sustainable production. Textile-making is no longer considered just decorative craft, but is an evolutionary and challenging discipline. New materials and technologies prompt me to frequently re-assess my work.

My concern is the replication of images in systems of order, or trying to make an object and even a colour repeat accurately. The serial repetition of these objects is what I use to form printed, surface patterns on silk and cotton. These surfaces can be constructed or deconstructed from one or more transparent layers of cloth, using devoré and discharge print techniques. The surface of a cloth can be laid with objects in repetitive formations, printed or applied.

Perfect People Print (1995)
screen printed pigmented and heat sensitised inks, acid dyed silk,
machine stitched and appliqued on cotton and linen cloth, buttons
137 x 231 cm

Patrick Snelling

My current work is focused on constructing pattern, using traditional and new techniques. I describe a journey, both physically and mentally, selecting objects on the way. Repetition, transparency, the layering of text, images, cloth and technology all form part of the process.

Separation from my family in the UK and starting out on another exploration in Australia have been very significant for me. When I come to a border I cross it.

The pieces hang and drape according to their respective textile properties. Some stiffened and others fluid, the series of panels have recurring motifs; the hand denotes the maker, the cross a form of indecision. The circle represents the world and the movement on it. Other symbols are associated with forms of travel.

As contemporary textile artists, we are constantly challenged to continue a textile tradition while absorbing new skills for dealing with emerging technologies. The use of converging methods provides me with an opportunity to collaborate with others outside my discipline and from around the world.

Recently I have been creating web site ideas for my own work; I see the site as an ongoing exhibition. The Internet now incorporates interactivity; shopping for textile goods and visiting virtual exhibitions of textiles around the world. As we face the future, textile practitioners are recognising the importance of this new technology which, until recently, has mainly been the domain of multi-media visual communicators.

I believe we should consider the economic, socio-political and democratic influences on the teaching of textiles in the 21st century. As a lecturer training students, I see good reasons for using Internet technology in our Art and Design curricula, and not just because it can be a rich visual and text-based medium. At the Royal Melbourne Institute of Technology we have an international Internet textile project whereby we can receive files from our global University partners, enabling staff and students to print fabrics digitally. Staff also use the web to develop on-line projects, displaying exhibition and teaching materials within our department. Email communication of course is very useful both locally and internationally with our exchange students in London and Italy. In a cash-starved university environment, these varied and expanding computer applications have helped in the very survival of the textile disciplines.

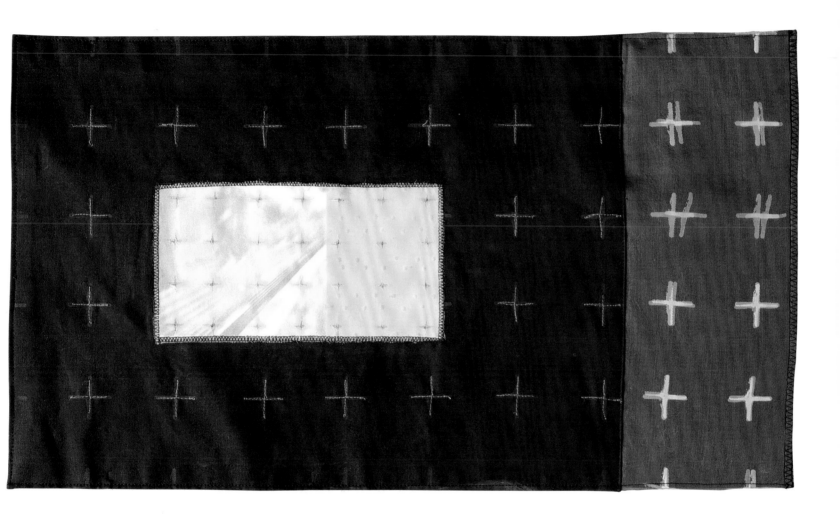

Metro Melbourne (1998)
screen printed pigmented inks,
thermal heat transfers,
CAD and machine stitching
59 x 33 cm

The computer is seductive; but is it a friend to creativity, or just a gimmick for the new generation of textile makers?

Patrick Snelling

This work has developed over a number of reworkings. The aim was to create a 3D effect on the fabric surface. The theme of *Flight* refers to my removal from one country to another; a migratory path leading to excursion, adventure and refuge. The topographical view of an Australian landscape is seen through the eyes of a European: sparse, open spaces with thin scrub and occasional water-holes. The cloth and images are in a state of flux with air currents and directional paths moving, rising and falling around my new world.

Flight (1997)
screen printed cotton deshuti, heat sensitive pigmented inks, eyelets, nylon tags, cotton tape, machine and hand stitches
182 x 145 cm

Born   1955 London, UK

Education

1976-81   MA & BA Degrees in Textiles, Manchester Metropolitan University, UK
          Nottingham Trent University
1993-94   Postgraduate Diploma in Applied Science; Museum Studies, Deakin University

Professional

          Lecturer Printed Textiles, RMIT University, Melbourne
          Member of the Design Institute of Australia

Selected Exhibitions

1994   *4th Australian Contemporary Art Fair*, Craft Victoria, Melbourne
          Sensibilities, Craft Victoria, Melbourne (solo)
          Crossing Borders, USA tour
1995   *Directions – Contemporary Cloth*, Crafts Council of ACT, Canberra
          ANCA Gallery, Textile and Cloth International Symposium, Canberra School of Art, ACT (solo)
1995-96   *Tradition, Cloth, Meaning*, Australia tour
1996   *Couture to Chaos*, National Gallery of Victoria, Melbourne
          Sydney and Crafts Council of the ACT, Canberra
          See the Light, Centre for Contemporary Craft, The Rocks
1998   *Hand to Cloth; Origins*, Metro Craft Centre, Melbourne
          Putting it in Print, Canberra, ACT and Nagano, Japan
          Origins and Perspectives, Contemporary Australian Textiles, Lodz, Poland
1999   *Drawn in Form*, Brisbane City Art Gallery

Collections

1988   University of Wollongong
1989   State Crafts Collection of Victoria
1989   The City of Melbourne
1990   The Commonwealth Bank of Australia
1993   The Jewish Museum of Australia
1994   National Gallery of Victoria

Publications

1992   *A Sense of Place; Contemporary Australian Embroidery*, Jerry Rodgers. Angus and Robertson, Australia ISBN 020 7169 78 0
1995   *International Textiles Yearbook*. Editor Mary Schoeser. Calmann & King, London ISBN 185 669 0725
1995   *Design and Practice for Printed Textile Design,* Andrea McNamara and Patrick Snelling, Oxford University Press ISBN 019 5533 71 2
1997   *The Body Image,* RMIT textile Internet collaboration. Craft Victoria Magazine Vol.27. *235. 82. pp20-24

Web site   http://minyos.its.rmit.edu.au/~rafps/poland.html

Patrick Snelling

From a distance, my work appears to have an easily recognisable meaning but, on close inspection, it reveals many surprises and a wealth of subtle details which take time to discover.

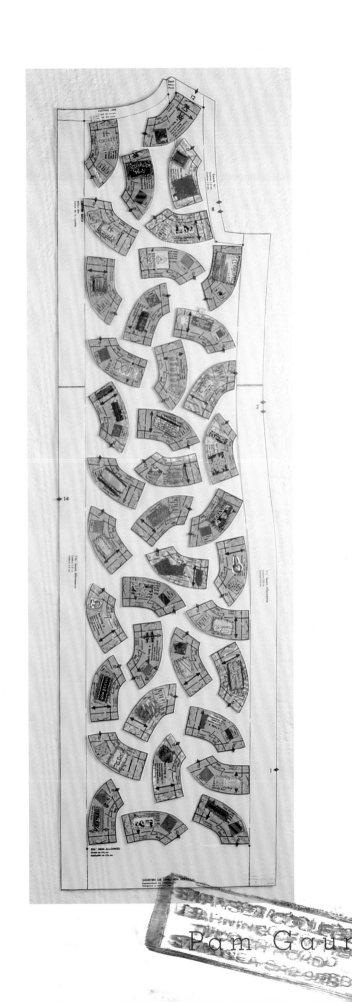

left:
Punto Tagliato (1997)
balsa wood, modelling paste, mixed media
assembled
191 x 149 cm

Red Dress-ed (1998)
photocopied draughting film, labels, fabric, thread etc
machine embroidery
124 x 40 cm

My mother was probably responsible for my current passion for textiles. I remember the linen cupboard with its carefully folded and stacked items, all of good quality. Some were for everyday use, and others only for special occasions. She was also responsible for teaching me how to knit when I was quite young, and how to make clothes from commercial patterns when I was a teenager. After my father died, she would spend time after work designing and painting posters to supplement our income, or simply for pleasure. She was always making something — miniature clothes for our dolls or puppets with detailed embroideries, nativity scenes modelled out of plaster, even including such things as spiders' webs made from thread.

As a teenager I was interested in fashion design as a career, but my mother tried to discourage me because she felt it was unlikely to be financially rewarding. However, I remained interested, and by the end of my degree in the early 1980s I was exploring body-related works. I didn't label these works 'fashion items' as they sat outside, or on the margins of, mainstream fashion. The pieces were constructed from machine-knitted sections that were then built on the body. My work was influenced to some extent by contemporary designers such as Issey Miyake and *Comme des Garcons*, with their innovative approaches to garment construction and their emphasis on the relationship between the body and the cloth. But with rather conservative Perth society, I couldn't foresee wide acceptance of such radical design.

Instead I began to explore possibilities with two dimensional stitched and collaged works. Eventually, these pieces became like large paintings which explored the illusion of depth through the processes of layering and collage. I would first dye and hand paint large pieces of fabric, these becoming my palette, then tear them up and reconstruct them. The sewing machine became a drawing tool that allowed me to explore the surface of the work and to embed in it small fragments of materials, such as dyed balsa wood, foil paper and little objects.

Another concern of my work is the reference to the history of textiles and the textile-making process. This interest in tradition, however, is always balanced by the inclusion of non-traditional materials and allusions to contemporary society. I am more interested in the compositional and structural elements of tradition than its technical aspects.

The stitch became the matrix of the work rather than the embellishment. On the one hand, the works contained fragile fragments, connected by almost nothing but stitch, yet their ethereal, diaphanous surfaces gave an illusion of depth. Since these early works, I have been intrigued by the qualities of old cloth and by the evocation of its own history through the surfaces, whether patched, stained, rich, worn, moth-eaten or faded. I wanted to create works which were contemporary equivalents of these old fragments of cloth.

Bead Baroque (1995) (detail)
fabric, thread, braid, buttons, light globes, bottle tops etc
hand and machine embroidery
43 x 26 cm

In the late 1980s my work went through a stage characterised by the deliberate exposure of the processes of textile-making which are traditionally hidden. Tacking stitches, seams, raw edges, fraying loose threads were shown for their inherent qualities. When a needle broke, I tied it into the work to make it something precious, rather than discarding it. In later works I have used a considerable number of broken needles as a form of embellishment. It is this kind of subversion of the conventional meaning of materials that I enjoy most. Transforming and elevating the discarded into the precious... using elements that appear familiar at first glance, but are in fact unconventional... teasing the viewer...

In 1992, after returning from study leave in north-west India, I felt so overwhelmed by the richness of that country's textile tradition that I decided to move in a new direction, away from the richly embroidered surfaces of my previous work.

Bodices and Facings (1994) (detail)
photocopied draughting film, thread, fabric,
broken needles etc
hand and machine embroidery
55 x 150 cm

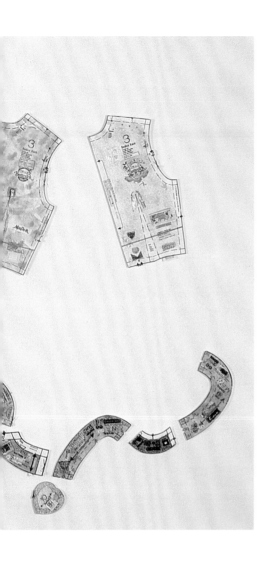

I began exploring the idea of 'borders' in all their permutations and became interested in the structure of European Renaissance lace. Thus lace and borders became a source of inspiration. At one level they offered ideas for the exploration of formats and shapes. I also found that the idea of margins and borders as 'non-centred' can be seen as an allusion to the marginalisation of textiles since the Industrial Revolution and its subordination to supposedly 'higher' media such as painting and sculpture. The border theme also made me consider another aspect of decoration. Whilst embellishment had always been a concern in my work, I began to research its relative scarcity — if not total absence — in contemporary Western art and society. This involved comparing the different levels of integration of ornamentation within the everyday life of different cultures. My research on this subject can perhaps explain the constant presence in my more recent works of strange and eclectic 'bits'; small things coming from Christmas bon-bons, hardware, electronic or haberdashery shops etc. The origin of these objects, whether they have been given, bought, found or inherited, is also relevant as it is part of their distinctive aura. The shapes of these small objects mirror aspects of the pattern motifs and by building them into the work I hope to encourage the viewer to question traditional and accepted notions of ornamentation. Since visiting India and researching the structure of Renaissance lace, I have worked with small units arranged into large pieces that occupy the corners or margins of spaces. From a distance these areas are intended to refer to textile fragments — carpets, lace, etc. On closer inspection, the viewer discovers they are individually different units and contain references to both traditional textiles and contemporary society. Each unit is thus a fragment that is part of a larger narrative.

At the same time I have been developing a separate strand of work which explores the language of fashion. These collages combine designer labels, care instruction labels and other references to the tools and processes of garment making. Each piece is laid over a support consisting of an enlarged reproduction of commercial pattern shapes. In some cases preference is given to the back of the label which is often visually more striking than the front. The dense and tight lay-out blurs the visual distinctiveness of the labels which lose their individuality and become small components of a larger whole. So the work combines 'floppy' engineering and coded structure of the pattern shapes with the appeal of the labels which reflect the fantasies of the potential consumer. One can also find references to mundane and repetitive domestic work as well as mythical and ideological meanings conveyed by contemporary fashion.

Pam Gaunt

Earlier works focused on the notion of 'memory and meaning', a theme which reflected my interest in aerial landscapes and maps, as well as architectural structures such as grids and scaffolding. Recently, I have tried to break away from the limitations of the predictable, traditional square/rectangle format.

Born 1952, Oldham, England
1963 came to Australia

Education
1979-82 BA Craft (Textiles), Western Australian Institute of Technology
1989 Graduate Diploma in Art and Design, Curtin University of Technology

Professional
Part-time Lecturer Fibre/Textiles, School of Art, Curtin University of Technology

Selected Exhibitions
1984 *Bodyworks*, Australian Craftworks Gallery, Sydney (solo)
1991 *Threads of Journeys* (international tour)
1994 *10th International Biennale Miniature Textiles*, Szombathely Museum, Hungary
1994 *In Our Hands*, Nagoya, Japan
1994 *One Size Fits Most, The Story So Far*, Perth, WA (solo)
1995 *Symbol and Narrative* (tour SE Asia)
1996 *Marginalia*, Perth Institute of Contemporary Arts (solo)
1997 *International Textiles Competition*, Museum of Kyoto, Kyoto, Japan
1998 *Nothing to Wear*, Distelfink Gallery, Melbourne

Commissions
1994/5 Banners (collaborative project) SAFTI Military Institute, Singapore
1995 Banner, Festival of Perth (Red Cross & WA Crafts Council)
1996 Banner, Perth City Council

Collections
Museum Fur Kunsthandwerk, Frankfurt am Main, Germany
Art Gallery of Western Australia
Jewish Museum of Australia
Crafts Board of the Australia Council
Curtin University of Technology
Ararat Regional Gallery, Victoria
Cruthers Collection

Publications
1992 *A Sense of Place, A National Overview of Contemporary Australian Embroidery,*
Jerry Rodgers/Angus & Robertson, ISBN 0 207 16978 0
1994 *Contemporary Embroidery*, Anne Morrell, Cassell, London ISBN 0 289 80105 2
1997 *Pam Gaunt – Selected Works 1989-97*, ISBN 1 86342 5144

Hearts on a Sleeve (1997)
photocopied draughting film,
fabric, thread, labels etc
machine embroidery
1240 x 620 mm

Pam Gaunt

Mungeribar refers to my affinity with stone – the medium my mother uses in her sculptures, while the threads and feathers signify my identity, simultaneously binding and flying.

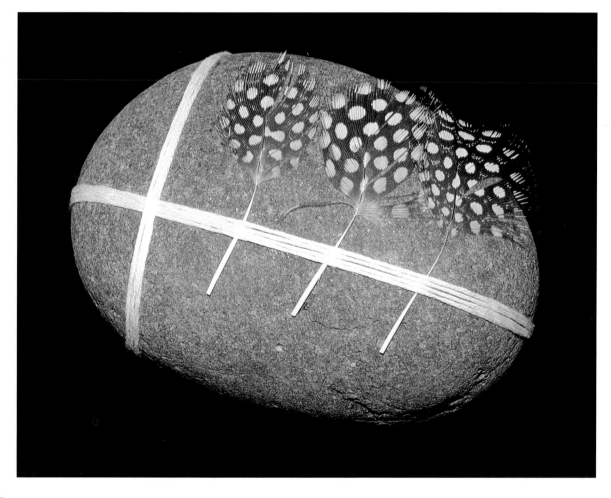

Mungeribar (1983)
river stone, cotton thread, guinea fowl feathers
width 35 cm

left:
Morning Spirits (1990)
painted muslin, bamboo, cotton threads
255 x 195 cm

Tori de Mestre

Becoming fully aware of the expressive potential of textiles was very important to me in my search for an identity. I had always wanted to be a painter. My mother is a sculptor and many family friends are painters and sculptors. There is no family tradition of making or collecting textiles. However, my mother did have several ball dresses from the 1940s tucked away in trunks. It was a delight to discover these beautiful fabrics: to hold her beads of amber, ivory, coral and silver, as well as the beaded African accessories. They were full of colour, texture and pattern and reminders of other personal histories.

A few years after studying painting in Sydney I moved to Melbourne. While training to be an art teacher in the mid-seventies I developed a greater interest in textiles, which offered potential beyond the rectangular, flat surface of the painter's canvas. I always wanted to extend the edges and distort the surface of my work. My first textile appliqué works were inspired by Matisse and Bonnard. They were figurative, rich in colour and pattern, and had an essential element of recycled fragments of fabrics. Gathering, saving, 'making-do' is a philosophy of living, not simply a necessity of hardship.

A significant change occurred during my camping trips in the Victorian National Parks, discovering the Flinders Ranges in South Australia – country dramatically different from that of the green coastal farmland of my childhood. I gathered sticks, stones, seed pods, feathers, all the while sketching and painting. The impact of the country was so great that I found it impossible to work in a figurative manner. After a period of distillation, the image was reduced to elements of colour and pattern in an attempt to reach the essence. I wanted to represent my emotional responses to the age of the country, to the different layers of natural and human histories.

Ready-made, coloured and patterned fabrics gave way to the use of muslin or gauze – painted, torn into strips, fragmented and then layered with sticks or feathers. Stitching was an integral part of the design, both structural and decorative; and later used as a metaphor for reconstructing eroded land. The pieces were made to hang without a frame, to fold or drape suspended away from the wall.

Rites of Spring is a celebration of regeneration in a desert country. Experience of the diverse nature of Australian land informs an investigation of duality – change and constancy, delicacy and harshness, ephemeral qualities and resilience.

Rites of Spring (1987)
painted muslin, cane cotton threads
2m x 3 m x 20 cm

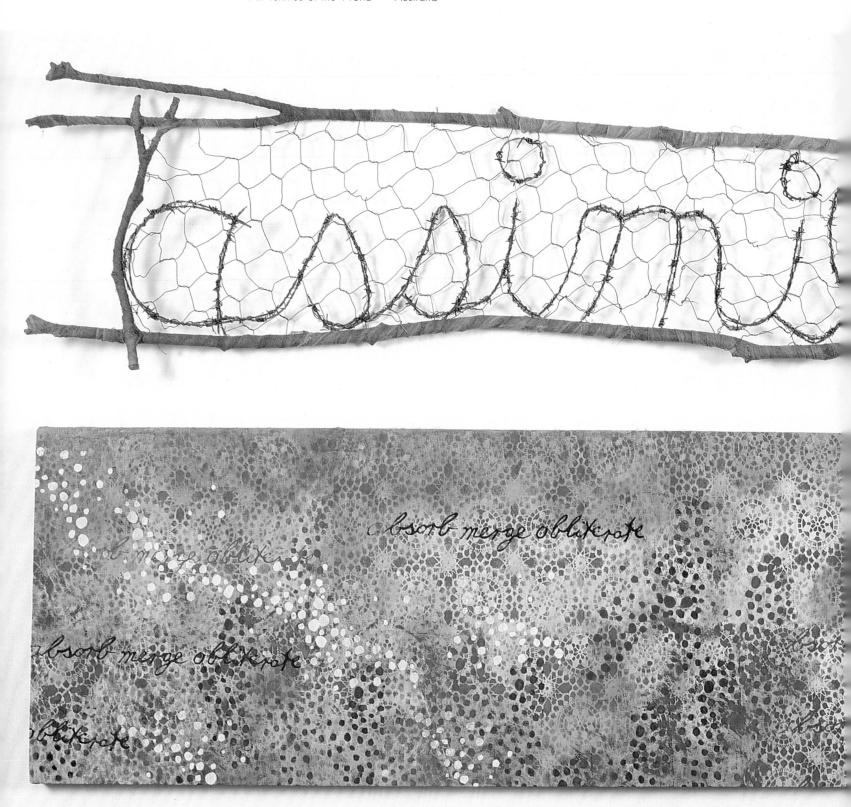

The *Civilise* series refers to the folly and fortitude of the settlers; the impact they had on the land, and the effect the land had upon them. 'Taming', 'Conquering' and 'Civilising' were frequent expressions used in response to the vast bush, where women worked alongside men.

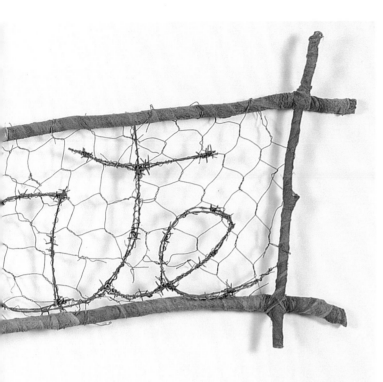

White Lies (1997)
eucalypt sticks, barbed wire, wire netting,
painted and printed muslin
100 x 180 cm

My interest in Aboriginal art and culture was intensified by seeing contemporary and dynamic work by women's groups in Aboriginal communities. *Morning Spirits* (page 62) tries to articulate at least some level of understanding of the spiritual connections to the land.

In 1990 I returned to live on the family farm but still kept the urge to work and travel. Recent journeys to India, Nepal, New Zealand, Japan and Bali were all experiences which influenced my work. The multitude of impressions and ideas need time and distance to sift and clarify. My enduring interest has been in nature and land; from early exotic gardens to desert landscapes.

I was also making small 2D and 3D constructions of bracken, fern or bamboo, bound with coloured cottons or painted strips of muslin, incorporating found natural objects. Three journeys to the Northern Territory during the late 80s and early 90s reinforced my need to express the spirit of the country. Recent works have been informed by my return to the childhood farm and local histories of the district. I have looked more personally at our dairy farm of the 50s and 60s. From old boxes I retrieved fragments of textiles as well as memories: cross-stitched gingham aprons, old linen chair covers, a velvet dress. I remembered the occasion of a vivid blue cotton dress printed with luscious ripe purple plums.

They became signs to my life story and it seemed timely to investigate the effect these objects had on my development as an artist. I commissioned a writer to help me with the catalogue. Gail Morgan's eloquent 'why this stubborn reclamation of the incidental...' leads to a happy recognition of the 'mystery of the ordinary' and 'the sacred disorder of memory'.

Tori de Mestre

Encroachment **represents the rapid invasion of European plants. Blackberry stains and thorns pierce the paperbark to signify the cost to native species. Old chimneys stand as a poignant reminder of the struggle for survival in climates so different from England.**

Encroachment (1993)
muslin, paperbark, thorns,
blackberry stains on canvas
167 x 76 cm

Born 1951 Wollongong, New South Wales

Education

1970-71 National Art School, Sydney (Fine Art)
1976-78 Melbourne State College, Diploma (Art)
1987 Australia Crafts/Council Board Overseas Study Tour
1991 Australia Council/Visual Art – Crafts Board, Artist-in-Residence, NT
1991-92 University of Wollongong, Masters Creative Arts, Visual/Textiles

Selected Exhibitions

1987 *13th International Tapestry Biennale*, Lausanne
1990 Christine Abrahams Gallery, Victoria (solo)
1991 Crafts Council Gallery, Northern Territory (solo)
1991-93 *Threads and Journeys*, Australian Quilt Textiles (international tour)
1992 Long Gallery, Wollongong University (MCA solo show)
1992 *Textiles and Praxis*, Craft West, Western Australia
1993 *Discerning Textiles*, Goulburn (national tour)
1995-96 *Crossing Borders*, University of Wollongong (USA tour)
1996 *Derivations*, Craft ACT (New Zealand tour)
1996 Project Contemporary Art Space (solo)
1997 Project Contemporary Art Space (solo)
1998 *Australian Textiles*, Lodz, Poland (tour)
1998 *Putting it in Print*, Craft ACT and Nara, Japan

Collections

University of Wollongong
Artbank
Melbourne University
Ararat Gallery
Stanthorpe Gallery
Australian Embassy, Washington DC

Commissions

Lismore Private Hospital, NSW
Corpus Christi College Chapel, Victoria
Bellevue Hotel, NSW
Benitos Restaurant, Victoria
Australian National, SA
Liverpool Hospital
Bankstown Lidcombe Hospital

Tori de Mestre

My tapestries are narratives of time and place. They represent geographic sites as well as cultural and theoretical viewpoints.

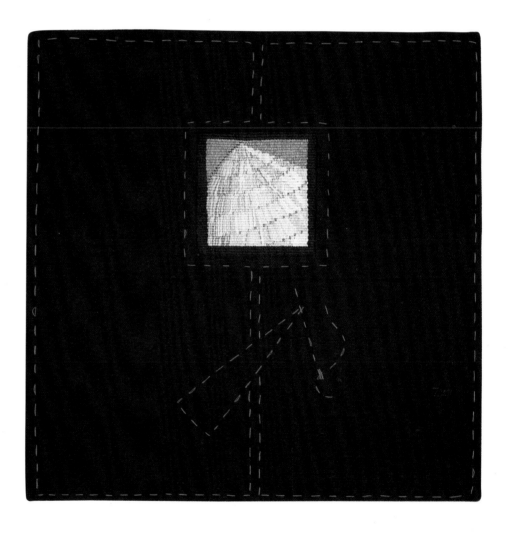

left:
Bushtucker/Junkfood – Goanna (1991)
tapestry set into collage/painted frame
50 x 40 cm

above:
Conical Hat and Palm Leaf (1996) (from *Hoa Tay* series)
tapestry inset into a hemp frame embroidered in cotton
30 x 30 cm

Valerie Kirk

I grew up on a farm in Dumfriesshire, Scotland with freedom to explore the fields, wood, loch and burn. I loved the countryside but could not wait to see the world. When I was seventeen I enrolled at the tapestry department of Edinburgh College of Art. In the 1970s Conceptual Art was strong and there was an emphasis on developing individual ideas with very little explanation of technique – we invented our own. The tapestries I wove were mainly grey and textured, reflecting the urban environment dulled by years of smoke and soot. While a student, I travelled through Canada and America, then on to Mexico to see the textiles and pyramids of Teotihuacan. I also worked and saved to see the major art collections in France and Spain, coming back enthused by large scale tapestries by Picasso, Tapies and Gaudi.

I came to Australia in 1979 to work as a weaver at the Victorian Tapestry Workshop in Melbourne. There we wove as a team translating Aboriginal paintings into tapestries commissioned for the Victorian Arts Centre. The collaborative process was always important in the workshops of Europe, but seemed directly opposite to the ethic of individualism I learned at Art College. I worked as part of the team, but missed the spontaneity possible in weaving my own designs.

My introduction to Aboriginal art stimulated a desire to see Papunya and the central desert of Australia. Several visits to the Red Centre and Aboriginal communities made a deep impression on me. Such an exotic experience for a Scot! The colour of the ground is the richest red and at sunset an entire landscape is engulfed in an intense warm light. *The Bushtucker/Junkfood* series developed from my experience at Kintore, Central Australia, where I taught silk painting. The young women who had gone to school in Alice Springs made bold drawings of buckets of chips and 'thickshakes' on the silk. The older women would draw in a traditional way, telling stories of waterholes, tracking animals and men and women sitting around campfires. On our days off, we went out to hunt for goannas and pussycat or to pick wild fruits. I was struck by the dichotomy of the modern shop offering local products such as kangaroo tails as well as every convenience food you would expect from a modern store. Hunting and gathering had become more of a recreation, and on a trip to the bush we might have a Fray Bentos meat pie along with roasted goanna. My tapestries mark the contrasts by using figurative elements showing the bushtucker, and collaged, painted frames representing the packaged food with wrappers which roll around the community in the dust and end up like paper mâché conglomerate.

I use drawing, collage and gouache painting to explore ideas before warping up to weave a tapestry. Large tapestries need a scaffolding-high warp loom, and metal or wooden frames are used for smaller works. My yarns come from many sources, including a local upholstery mill, as Australian wool is very soft and refined – good for fine Italian knitwear, but it packs down too much in tapestry.

I am still attracted to the Scottish wools with their subtle blends of colour in a coarse texture. I now work in a flat weave, but the surface quality remains important – the sheen of a mercerised cotton or the raw quality of a rough linen can add a rich visual texture to the piece.

Pineforest Quilt – Applied, Used, Discarded (1995)
woven tapestry
90 x 150 cm

My first solo exhibition in Australia was titled *Opals and Images of Outback Australia* and this was a culmination of months spent travelling around Australia with sketchbooks, a small tapestry frame and a bag of assorted yarns. Two small works, *Opals* and *Luck*, capture the age and superstitions associated with the opal. When they became popular as jewellery, the diamond industry promoted the myth that opals were unlucky unless set with diamonds. The fossils in the centre of the tapestry were drawn in Adelaide Museum where I saw a complete set of opals shaped like the vertebrae of a *plesiosaur*. *Opals and Dinosaur Bones* has a raw sense of colour conveying the harsh conditions of the mining areas; but it is also an organised composition reflecting the human relationship to land and its mineral resources.

In recent years, regular tours to Vietnam have led to a new series, *Hoa Tay* or Flower Hand. The Vietnamese language has endowed the hand with an evocative name, which literally means flower-hand. It describes the flowing hands of the dancer, or the potter's hands giving form to clay, the dextrous hands of a farmer or the hands of a sculptor imparting soul to the wood. In Vietnam a vast amount of work is carried out by hand — villages of people making baskets, men sitting at Jacquard looms in their homes, weaving silk, or women embroidering beside a path high up in the mountains.

My tapestries are narratives of place, time and a personal viewpoint. They represent geographic sites as well as cultural and political viewpoints from a Northern/Southern hemisphere perspective. When I first came to this country, a friend commented that I depicted Australia like a British garden, and drew an analogy with the first Western artists and explorers. I am reminded of the old Indian tale of two friends, one of whom stays at home and tends his garden and the other who travels the world. In later life they meet and realise they have come to know the same things. As a child I knew my surroundings through constant contact and renewal. In adult life I have explored a wider world and my art has provided a point of reflection; but in different ways the process has been about understanding, learning, developing a familiarity and making sense of the world.

I settled for three months in Busselton WA, and set up a larger loom to weave *Opals: Coober Pedy,* an image which combines a map of the mining area with details of the ground on the Mullock heaps where tourists look for opals. I stared for hours into the churned earth, searching for the 'fire in the stone'. The odd piece of rock with a smooth coloured area could be found – non-precious but fascinating. True gems show flashes of colour within glass-like forms. From a small painted cartoon I made a line drawing to scale, placing this behind a number 12 warp. I worked steadily over the next eight weeks to produce the tapestry. Colours from dust and intense heat contrasted with the lustrous threads, evoking the iridescent semi-precious stone.

Opals: Coober Pedy (1985)
woven tapestry
155 x 110 cm

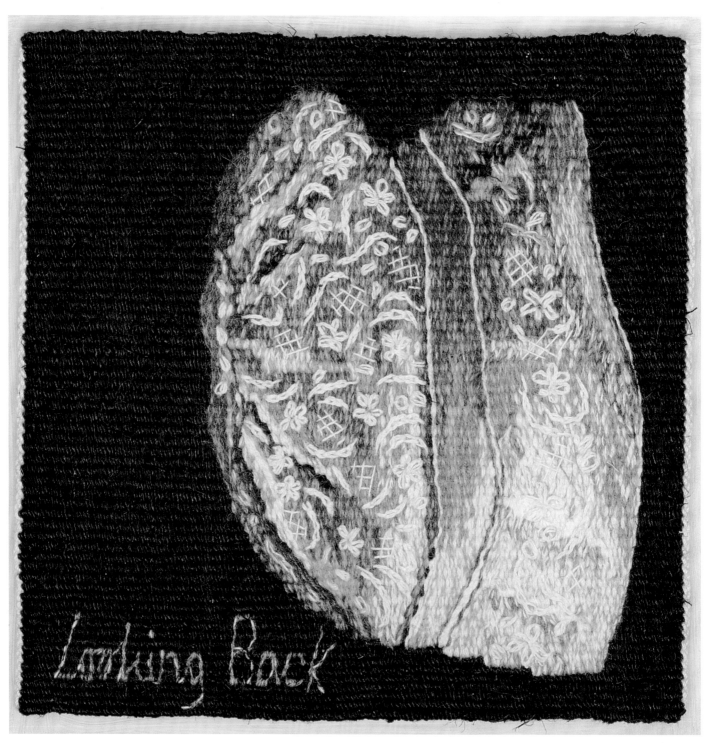

At present I am working on a series of small tapestries called *Looking Forward – Looking Back*. These deal with my thoughts since having children, looking forward to their future and seeing them grow and change so quickly as well as thinking back to my own childhood. The continuity of generations within a family has become more obvious and more important, but I am acutely aware of my girls' separation from their Scottish family and a culture which is so much part of me. In the work, black and white mark the contrasts and divide, while patterns from Ayrshire needlework used in babies' bonnets and christening gowns reflect a nostalgia and longing.

People have always said to me 'You must have a lot of patience to do tapestry'; but the real strengths needed are vision and determination, not simply passive endurance. In its simplest form, tapestry is like darning a sock – anyone can do it; but tapestry is not just about technique. Although I like the rhythm, the sound of bobbins and the physical aspect of tapestry weaving, it is the escape into another world of image making that I enjoy the most.

Born   1957 Dumfries, Scotland

Education and Awards
1974-79	BA, Art & Design, Postgraduate, Edinburgh College of Art
1978	Andrew Grant Travel Award. Helen Rose Bequest Prize. HRH Prince Charles Award of Merit
1979-80	Art Teachers' Certificate, Goldsmiths' College, University of London

Selected Exhibitions
1990	*Opals and Images of Outback Australia*, Warnambool Art Gallery (solo)
1994	*International Encounter of Miniature Tapestry*, Mexico City (tour)
1996	*12th Tamworth Fibre Textile Biennial,* Tamworth, NSW
1996	*It's About Time*, Portland, USA
1996	*Capital Works*, Takashimaya Gallery, Singapore and the University of Hong Kong Gallery
1997	Salon Natasha, Hanoi, Vietnam
1998	*Origins and New Perspectives: Contemporary Australian Textiles*, Łodz, Poland
	Dwelling Street Theatre, Canberra (solo)

Selected Collections

Powerhouse Museum, Sydney
Ararat Regional Gallery, Victoria
Kensington Swann, New Zealand
Shipley Museum and Art Gallery, GB
Edinburgh School of Art, GB
Cumbria School of Art & Design, GB

Professional

Senior Lecturer & Head of Textiles, Australian National University, Canberra School of Art
Convenor of SHIFT Symposium, Contemporary Textiles – Towards the next Millennium, ANU
Tour Leader and Textiles Lecturer, Cultural Tours to Vietnam

Selected Publications

FiberArts Design Book 5, 1995
FiberArts Magazine 1993, 96
International Tapestry Journal 1993, 97, 98

Website

www.anu.edu.au/ITA/CSA/textiles.html

left:
Looking Back (1997)
tapestry and embroidery, wool and cotton
20 x 20 cm

Valerie Kirk

As I look back on my life so far, I can see subtle connections between the physical activities of dyeing or stitching, and my perceptions of the world expressed in poetry. I chose the title *Poet of Cloth* to suggest this integration. This garment (right) is one of a series commissioned by the Art Gallery of New South Wales for *The Fauves* exhibition in 1996.

right:
Poet of Cloth: The Fauves (1996)
silk organza, shibori techniques
commissioned by the Art Gallery of NSW,
Sydney, in conjunction with *The Fauves*
exhibition

left:
Luminous Bardo (1995) (detail)
silk organza, shibori technique

Patricia Black

I can pinpoint my initiation into the realm of textiles, recalling memories of great aunts engaged in time-consuming handwork; watching my mother's meticulous tailoring, as she had watched her own mother before; undergoing a gradual apprenticeship in the texture and drape of fabrics.

A pivotal point in my career was when I joined *The Designers' Collective* in Adelaide. This group was founded by Tricia Hanlon and Jenni Dudley, both artists trying to promote limited-edition and unique, wearable pieces. This genre became increasingly difficult to promote during a conservative era in the Eighties when fashion reverted to safe basic black, and eccentric clothing was no longer 'hip'. So I moved to Sydney, hoping to find work in theatrical costume, and hoping to gain recognition within a broader artistic community.

Armed with an article in the Australian textile magazine *Textile Forum* and a few samples of my work, I approached the Crafts Council of New South Wales. Happily, my work was accepted, and this led to exhibitions and invitations to work with other craftspeople, such as Giordano and Cooney, makers of leather masks.

An appointment as the NSW Member of the Craft Council in 1991 gave me an insight into local politics as well as a rapport with craftspeople working in other media. Later there were opportunities offered by supportive organisations such as Craft Australia to promote work in the USA, which enabled me to contact the few galleries sympathetic to small-production designers. However, the strongest overseas pull for me had always been Italy, and particularly Venice.

Meanwhile, in 1992 the opportunity to learn shibori led me to Nagoya, Japan, where I took part in the World Shibori Conference. I had an idea of the possibilities of shibori after Inga Hunter's Textile Forum workshop in 1989. In Nagoya, resist-dyeing has now reached an astonishingly high level of technical virtuosity. The World Shibori Network commissioned me to transform a traditional kimono using adapted techniques.

The discharged and pleated folds of the transparent silk organza reminded me of radiating bursts of energy. While working on this piece I was reading *The Tibetan Book of the Dead*. The 'bardo' is the state after death when the soul passes through waves of energy.

Luminous Bardo (1995) (detail)
silk organza, shibori technique

Organic forms are created by certain shibori processes. Manipulating the fabric gives it new energy. The water swells the fabric, which then unfolds to delight the creator's eye.

It is the element of uncertainty in the process of shibori that fascinates me. I always enjoy that moment of sweet anticipation when an unpredictable soggy piece of fabric is opened up to reveal a wonderful pattern or texture. The three-dimensional pieces seem to form shapes of their own, naturally adapting to the contours of the body, hence their suitability for dance. My cloth is sometimes bound with twine, clamped with various shapes or even imprinted with plastic champagne corks. In fact, all kinds of weird and wonderful experimentation takes place!

I found an opportunity to present my work in the *New Zealand Wearable Art Awards*. This event is made possible by sculptress and organiser Suzie Moncrieff, with her sister Heather and the community of Nelson in New Zealand's South Island. It is a spectacular environment that encourages the creation of adventurous, uncompromising work.

I also began professional costume work with the dance company *Darc Swan*. This included a children's fairy tale production commissioned by the Bennelong Trust at the Sydney Opera House. In the following years I collaborated with American Choreographer Anneta Luce on many productions. In line with her belief that a broader audience should be exposed to dance, unconventional venues were chosen for many of the productions. In addition to the work of designing costumes, I was also given the opportunity to create large textile sculptures that could serve as set designs – these had to be easily transportable. The costumes, or 'body sculptures' as I think of them, can be seen as a second skin responding to corporal motion. The 3D pieces, when worn, echo the motion of the body; the pleats bounce and the spikes stretch and extend the dancer's contortions. Dancers tell me that wearing the body sculptures enhances their perceptions of their body movements so that there is a dynamic rapport – perhaps it is the energy of the physical manipulation of the cloth that is somehow imparted to the wearer.

In 1995 at the *American Surface Design Conference* in Portland, USA, I participated in a workshop with shibori dyer Kaei Hayakawa, and Yoshiko Wada, the driving force behind the World Shibori Network, and co-author of *The Definitive Book of Shibori*. It deepened my understanding of the process of imprinting 'memory' onto textile, as well as pattern and colour, with three-dimensional results. Eager to experiment, I began a series of work in collaboration with glass artist Alan Prowd using internal light sources: we exploited the translucent, changing effects of illumination through silk organza.

View from the Antipodes (1997)
body sculpture
Itajiame shibori, manual pleating on
silk organza
12m x 1.5m
Dancer: Anneta Luce

Patricia Black

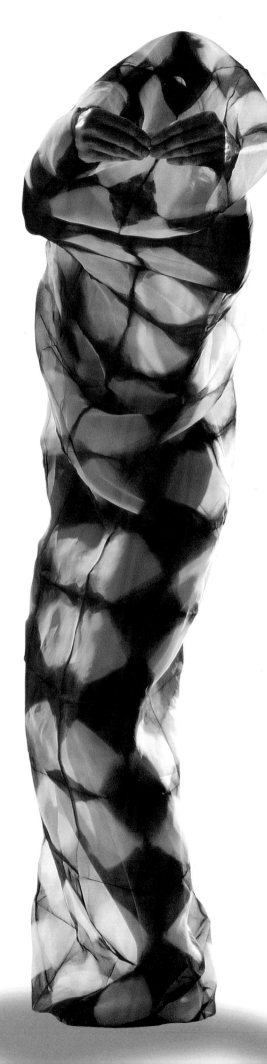

Ferrous Extrusion *(see back cover)*

This bound type of 'kumo shibori' with the three dimensional peaks imprinted in the silk by using heat and steam, was dyed initially using natural processes; the fabric has been bound, then wrapped in a piece of rusty iron, a pole in a Venetian canal in fact. After a week it was still there, with the tides acting as a solution and the salt water as a mordant. This use of rust derives from the ancient printmaking technique of Emiglia Romana.

In 1996 a breakthrough came in the shape of a residency in Besozzo, North Italy. This resulted in many professional opportunities, including workshops in Venice and Tuscany. The culmination was a commissioned modern dance performance on the Feast of *La Befana* (the Good Witch) at the costume museum of Venice, the *Palazzo Moncenigo*. I remember that day very well: up to my elbows in dye at the workshop on Giudecca, dressing in hastily grabbed finery, dashing along the foggy pathways of Venice to a genuine 16th-century *palazzo*, like Cinderella – late for the Ball. The pumpkin coach was a Venetian *vaporetta*, but I wasn't complaining!

Back in Australia, I participated in a touring exhibition of the work of students of shibori Master Hiroyuki Shindo and his wife Chikako. I also worked on a commission from the Art Gallery of NSW for their *Dancing to the Flutes* Exhibition in celebration of Indian art and sculpture, with live music performed by Indian musicians. In 1997 I returned to Italy, and as part of a group project, we mounted a shibori installation along the Grand Canal in Venice.

Links with Japanese organisations continue with a commission to dye specially woven silk and create a 'fashion' garment for the permanent collection of the Gumna Silk Corporation.

As a textile artist at the end of the 20th century, I have discovered that shibori is a perfect textile craft, never seriously threatened by industrial imitation. I believe in the 'grass roots' notion that the process is as important as the product. My ambition is to nurture others involved in the activity of textiles made by hand.

left:
Eclipse of the Square Moon (1998)
Itajime shibori, 'Leno' silk
Dancer: Anneta Luce

This piece was commissioned by the
Gumna Silk Corporation, Japan for their
Fashion Collection 1998

Born   1956 Murray Bridge, South Australia

Education and Awards
1975-77   Flinders University, South Australia (BA)
1977-78   Kingston CAE (Grad Dip Ed)
1993   Overall Design Award, New Zealand Wearable Art Awards
1994-95   Winner Silk Section, New Zealand Wearable Art Awards
1997   Highly Commended, New Zealand Wearable Art Awards
1997   Studio Residency, Bessozo, Italy; Australia Council

Selected Exhibitions
1987   Craftspace, The Rocks, Sydney
1988   Craftspace, The Rocks, Sydney (solo)
1991   *Dressed to Kill*, Australian National Gallery, Canberra
                 Takisada Department Store, Nagoya, Japan
1993   *Below the Surface*, Goulburn Regional Gallery, NSW
                 Newcastle Art Gallery, NSW (solo)
1994   *Wearables*, Palos Verdes Art Center, Los Angeles, USA
                 Fashion Shibori, International Shibori Symposium, Ahemabad, India
1994-98   *San Francisco Gift Fair*, Craft Australia, USA
1997   Palazzo Moncenigo, Venice, Italy (solo)
1998   *Artisan*, Edinburgh Arts Festival, Edinburgh, GB (solo)
                 Textilhemp, St Polten, Austria

Commissions
1986   *Fur & Feathers*, Museum of South Australia
1991   *Civilisation*, Australia National Gallery
1992   Takeda Corporation, International Shibori Symposium, Nagoya, Japan
1993   Pompeii, Australian Museum, Sydney
1994   *In a Tribal Tide,* Powerhouse Museum, Sydney
1995-96   *Fauve, Dancing to the Flutes*, Art Gallery of New South Wales
1997   Gunma Silk Corporation, Japan
1998   *Te Papa,* New Zealand Wearable Art Company

Selected Workshops
1992 & 98   Tutor, Batik & Surface Design Association of Australia
1993-94   Tutor, Textile & Fibre Arts Association of Australia
1996   Tutor, Instituto D'Arte, Padova, Italy
1998   Tutor, Commune di Venezia, Castello, Venezia

Patricia Black

In parts of the Australian landscape the sense of space is so strong that you can almost touch it. I tried to make this piece *(below)* appear as insubstantial as possible, as if it's not quite there. The woven pieces are actually quite strong, but I like this contradiction.

an inner garden: embroidering on air (1993)
plant fibres, sand, air
approx. 250 x 500 x 900 cm

left:
Sampler for Lucy Beedon (1998) (detail)
plant-dyed cloth, teatowel, shells, thread
54 x 35 cm

Ruth Hadlow

I never know where to start talking about my work because it goes in so many directions. I used to think that maybe I was fickle and that sooner or later I would settle down and concentrate in one direction, but now I don't worry. I just get on with making it.

Some of my work is about landscape. When I first crossed the Nullabor, over to Western Australia, I realised how much your own sense of landscape is built into you from an early age. The space out there was so exhilarating, and I think my response to it comes from the open flat red country of my early childhood in the Mallee, even though when I was seven we moved to Canberra among the green-grey mountains. I've read that colonial explorers found that huge expanse depressing and even claustrophobic, which amazes me.

An inner garden: embroidering on air is a piece about that inland space. On one level it is concerned with the relationships between gardens and textiles and plants. There are references to Persian garden carpets and the 17th-century French gardens based on embroidery patterns; but mainly it is about space; about the space that is so strong in parts of the country that it's tangible. I am intrigued by the fact that because we can't see that space and have difficulty describing it, we don't believe in it; and yet when you're out in the bush it is so potent that it's impossible to ignore. I guess I think of it as a metaphor for the spirit, and want to find ways to work with it despite its lack of substance. I tried to make this piece appear as insubstantial as possible, as if it's not quite there. The woven pieces are actually quite strong, but I like the contradiction. With a lot of the sculptural work I'm playing with things like substance and deception.

I've been trying for quite a while to find ways of making pieces about landscape that aren't based on European painting traditions. It's to do with understanding the Australian environment in a way that is about belonging here and being familiar with it. I'm trying to express ideas through intimate perceptions, through the senses. I work with small details, and materials that are specific to certain places, while at the same time acknowledging my own cultural histories.

Travel Wagga (1997-98)
leaves, thread
approx. 200 x 90 cm

The leaves came from different parts of the country: Roaring Beach, Lake Mungo, Wybalenna... the leaf pieces are a record of these places and of the experience of being there. The piece is based on the quilts which were made during the Depression out of samples of men's suits and hessian sacks.

Ruth Hadlow

Most of my work refers to various traditions and histories of textiles, whether I am making sculpture, embroidery or installation work. I think of those traditions as my blood lines, my family history. I started embroidery seriously after I badly damaged my wrists while weaving large sculptures – I developed repetitive strain injury. I wasn't able to make anything for months and became very depressed. It felt as if I'd lost my whole life. I had to stop making large-scale work for a while and find other ways of doing things.

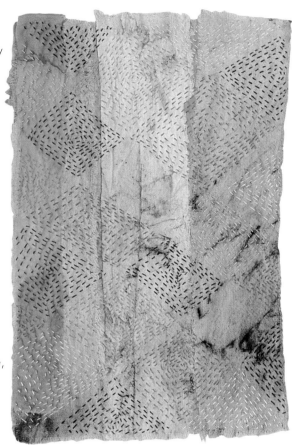

I love the way embroidery is just like drawing, but specific to cloth. I never draw on the cloth first, I just work directly with the needle and thread. The uneven stitches the hand makes, the peculiar lines and shapes, all seem to be part of the nature of it. I often try to find ways to be less in control so there is more of that unknown factor in a piece. With different types of work I set up various ways to subvert my need to be able to predict, to be safe.

Sometimes I use mola techniques in embroideries, cutting back through layers of patterned fabrics so I never quite know what part of a pattern I'm going to reveal. Other times I dye cloth, using lots of layers of plant dyes and mordants over each other, with simple shibori techniques to create patterns. After a while, complex reactions happen between the different layers and I don't have any idea what will come out of the dye bath. The *Mungo Samplers* were made like that, boiling up different leaves each day in a billy on the fire during a camping trip. It keeps the balance of an image half in my hands and half unknown. I'm in control to the extent that I set up the structure and know what the piece is about, but there's room for some kind of dialogue along the way that keeps the work lively. I am fascinated by the familiarity of cloth, and the historical references that are built into certain fabrics or objects. While I was having acupuncture treatment for my wrists, I came across some wonderful 19th-century pincushions with messages or homilies written on their surfaces with pinheads. Apparently they were given as commemorative presents for births or christenings and were purely ornamental. And there I was – a human pincushion with these big needles sticking into each wrist.

A whole series of works developed, using pins and pincushions, exploring ideas about pain, decoration and the creative impulse. *Portrait: Fate or Fortune* is one of those: I was asking questions such as what was I doing to my body, how much my sense of self was bound up in the process of making, and to what extent is the need to create integral to being human?

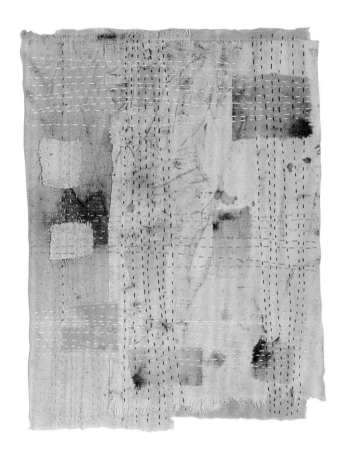

Cape Barren Samplers 5 – 7 (1996-98)
found cloth, plant and mineral dyed
cloths, thread
approx. 30 x 20 cm each

The Cape Barren Samplers **are part of a group of works made in response to an island in Bass Strait. On a beach called** *Thunder and Lightning* **I found a wonderful piece of scruffy old stained cloth. I've been tearing it up and making small embroideries, trying to evoke in an abstract way a sense of the space, and the basic quality of existence on those islands. I'm also referring to the** *kantha* **quilts from Bengal and India, made of worn-out saris stitched together, and to** *kuba* **cloths, the raffia embroideries from Zaire, which are so restrained in their colours and patterning.**

Ruth Hadlow

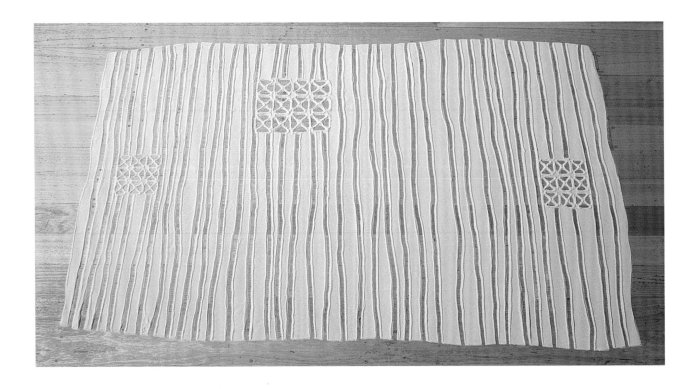

Having to change the way I worked turned out to be quite liberating. I realised that I could explore more widely, concentrating on ideas rather than techniques. I really appreciate not trying to sell my work. I make a living from several other things, including designing for the theatre, working on scripts with playwrights, teaching workshops, and community arts projects. They're all things I enjoy and which stretch me creatively. When I get back to my own work I feel I can really indulge myself after all the compromises and negotiations involved in collaborating with others. I enjoy the balance of work I have now.

Some of my favourite work is the least permanent, the ephemeral installation pieces. They are often made from materials found in the environment, like *Sand Carpet,* existing only for a brief period in a particular place. The opportunities to work like this are quite rare as it's not commercial and, of course, the pieces can't be in touring exhibitions. Usually the only chance to make this kind of work is during residencies when there is space and time and no expectation of something permanent at the end.

In the end I guess I just love making things, discovering as I go what I'm making and why. It's such an adventure.

The process of making the ephemeral pieces allows me to work through ideas quite quickly in a very fresh way, exploring and making discoveries as I go. It is very direct like drawing, but more interesting for me because of the energy of the physical presence of the object. I think there's also another kind of energy that exists because of the short life-span of the pieces – they have an intensity like that of a butterfly.
And the fragility of the work somehow seems much more real to me than things that might last forever. It's such a forgiving medium; if you don't like something you can just sweep it up and start again. Which constantly reminds me that there are always 10 million possibilities, any of which could be wonderful...

Sand Carpet (1997)
200 x 100 cm

Born   1963 Swan Hill, Victoria

Education and Awards

1990   BA in Visual Arts, Edith Cowan University, Perth
1993   Artist-in-Residence, Jam Factory Craft and Design Centre, Adelaide
1994   Artist-in-Community, City of Clarence, Hobart
1995   Professional Development Grant, Arts Tasmania
1997   Artist-in-Residence, Moonah Arts Centre, Hobart
1998   Artist-in-Residence, Noosa Regional Gallery
1998   Professional Development Grant, Australia Council

Selected Exhibitions

1993   *an inner garden: embroidering on air*, Jam Factory Craft and Design Centre, Adelaide (solo)
1994   *High Fibre Diet*, Fremantle Arts Centre, Perth
1994   *Reveal/Conceal*, Artspace, Adelaide
1995   *The Meaning of Dress*, Tasmanian Museum and Art Gallery, Hobart
1995   *Dualisms # 2*, Devonport Art Gallery (national tour)
1995   *Tradition, Cloth, Meaning*, Long Gallery, Hobart (national tour)
1996   *Second Look, Prospect Textile Biennial*, Adelaide (national tour)
1996   *Out of The Linen Closet – Artist Embroiderers*, Moonah Arts Centre, Hobart
1997   *Transparent*, Dick Bett Gallery, Hobart (solo)
1998   *Ecologies of Place and Memory*, Plimsoll Gallery, Hobart (national tour)

Selected Freelance Teaching

1994   *Fibre Skills* Camping Workshop for Tasmanian Aboriginal women, co-teaching with Gwen Egg
1994   *Fibre-Net-Works* Workshop, co-teaching with Nalda Searles, Fremantle Arts Centre, Perth
1997   *Fibre Masterclass*, co-teaching with Gwen Egg, Moonah Arts Centre, Hobart
1997   *Concept, Collaboration, and Installation*, Tamworth Textile Masterclass, Tamworth
1998   *Subverting the Template Masterclass*, Moonah Arts Centre, Hobart
1998   *Exploring Ideas through Making*, Shift Textile Symposium, Canberra Art School
1998   *Sensibilities of Place*, Tamworth Textile Masterclass, Tamworth

Selected Commissions

1995   *Desires*, co-design and construction with Greg Methé, Terrapin Theatre
1996   *No Time Like The Present*, co-devise and design, Two Turns Dance Project
1997   *The Fork*, co-design and construction with Greg Methé, Terrapin Theatre
1998   *One*, co-devise and design for solo dance piece with Joanna Pollitt

Collections

          Museum & Art Gallery of the NT, Darwin

Ruth Hadlow

Acknowledgements

Sue Rowley would like to thank Diana Wood Conroy and Gillian McCracken for advice and support.
Footnotes to essay:

1. Doreen Mellor, 'Australian Indigenous textiles: facilitating radical change',
    Re-inventing Textiles: Tradition and Innovation in Contemporary Practice, ed. Sue Rowley,
    Telos, Winchester UK, 1999,
    see also Doreen Mellor, 'Exploring the dynamics of surface and origin: Australian Indigenous textile and fibre practice',
    Origins and New Perspectives — Contemporary Australian Textiles, ed. Glenda King,
    Queen Victoria Museum and Art Gallery and Craft Australia, Launceston, Tasmania, 1998, pp. 25-6.

2. See *47th Venice Biennale exhibition catalogue, Fluent,* ed. Hetti Perkins, Art Gallery of New South Wales,
    Sydney, 1997.

3. Gillian McCracken, 'Many Voices', *Many Voices: 13th Tamworth Fibre Textile Biennial,* Tamworth City Gallery,
    Tamworth, New South Wales, 1998, p. 4.

4. Diana Wood Conroy, 'Solvig Baas Becking: a sense of infinite order', *Object*, 3:94, p. 29.

5. Peter Dormer (ed.), *The Culture of Craft: Status and Future*, Manchester University Press, Manchester and New
    York, 1997.

6. Andrea McNamara and Patrick Snelling, *Design and Practice for Printed Textiles*, Oxford University Press,
    Melbourne, 1995.

7. Jennifer Isaacs, *The Gentle Arts: 200 Years of Australian Women's Domestic and Decorative Arts*, Lansdowne,
    Willoughby, New South Wales, 1987;
    Grace Cochrane, *The Crafts Movement in Australia: A History*, UNSW Press, Sydney, 1992;
    Joan Kerr (ed.), *Heritage: The National Women's Art Book*, Art & Australia, Sydney, 1995.

8. Jim Logan, 'Towards a definition of Australian folk art', exhibition catalogue, *Everyday Art: Australian Folk Art*,
    National Gallery of Australia, Canberra, 1998, p. 9.

Selected further reading:

Crossing Borders, Contemporary Australian Textile Art
Ed Sue Rowley, publ. University of Wollongong, Australia ISBN 0 86418 330 5

Dreaming, the Art of Aboriginal Australia
Peter Sutton, Viking Publication, 1988 ISBN 0670824496

Peintres Aborigenes d'Australie, ed. Sylvie Crossman & Jean-Pierre Barou
Indigene Editions, Parc de la Villette, Paris 1998

Wearable Art – Design for the Body
Craig Potton Publishing, New Zealand 1996 ISBN 0 908802 34 X

Patricia Black refers to:
Shibori:The Inventive Art of Shaped Resist Dyeing, Wada, Rice & Barton, Kodansha Press, 1998

Translation of Elytis poetry by M.K.

Book retail outlets

Worldwide
Telos Art Publishing (mail order)
PO Box 125 Winchester
England SO23 7UJ
Fax ++44 (0)1962 864 727
www.telos.net
telos@dial.pipex.com

Great Britain
Crafts Council of Great Britain
Gallery Shop (mail order)
Tel ++44 (0)171 806 2557
Fax ++44 (0)171 837 6891

Contemporary Applied Arts
Tel ++44 (0)171 436 2344
Fax ++44 (0)171 436 2446

Germany
Textil Forum Service
Tel +49 (0)511 817 006
Fax +49 (0)511 813 108
tfs@ETN-net.org

Australia
The Australian Forum for Textile Arts
Tel ++ 61 (0) 7 3300 6491
Fax ++ 61 (0) 7 3300 2148
tafta@uq.net.au

Artisan Craft Books, Melbourne
Tel ++ 61 (0)3 9329 6042
Fax ++ 61 (0)3 9326 7054

Japan
Gallery Gallery, Kyoto
Tel ++81 (0)75 341 1501
Fax ++81 (0)75 341 1505

ART TEXTILES OF THE WORLD

An illustrated series of profiles of outstanding contemporary artists working in a variety of textile media:

Art Textiles of the World: Great Britain Volume 2
Ed. Dr Jennifer Harris, Whitworth Art Gallery, Manchester
including Polly Binns, Michael Brennand-Wood, Caroline Broadhead, Jo Budd, Shelley Goldsmith, Alice Kettle, Janet Ledsham, Lesley Mitchison
ISBN 0 9526267 6 4 (Oct 1999)

Art Textiles of the World: USA
including Kyoung Ae Cho, Virginia Davis, Deborah Fisher, Ann Hamilton, Linda Hutchins, Charlene Nemec Kessell, Jane Lackey, Susan Lordi Marker, Jason Pollen, Jane Sauer
ISBN 0 9526267 1 3   (2000)

Art Textiles of the World: Japan
Masae Bamba, Machiko Agano, Yasuko Fujino, Masashi Honda, Haruko Honma, Masakazu and Naomi Kobayashi, Kiyonori Shimada, Hiroyuki Shindo, Yuko Takada, Chiyoko Tanaka, Mitsuo Toyazaki, Chiyu Uemae
128pp, 118 col. illus.
ISBN 0 9526267 4 8 (1997)

Art Textiles of the World: Great Britain
Jeanette Appleton, Jo Barker, Kate Blee, Sara Brennan, Dawn Dupree, Sally Greaves-Lord, Nicola Henley, Greg Parsons, Marta Rogoyska, Lynn Setterington
112pp, 103 col. illus.
ISBN 0 9526267 2 1 (1996)

REINVENTING TEXTILES
supported by Southern Arts Association
A new series of cutting-edge essays from around the world:

Volume 1: Tradition and Innovation in Contemporary Practice
ed. Prof. Sue Rowley
contributors: Julian Ruesga Bono, Hazel Clark, Diana Wood Conroy, Wlodimierz Cygan, Janis Jefferies, Doreen Mellor, Margo Mensing, Zahke Ngqobe, Marian Pastor Roces, Nima Poovaya-Smith, TK Sabaparthy, Maria Teresa Guerrero, Malgorzata Wroblewska-Markiewicz
ISBN 1 9020150 0 2   (1999)

ALSO AVAILABLE
Take 4 – new perspectives on the British art quilt
published in association with the Whitworth Art Gallery
Edited with an introduction by Dr Jennifer Harris
essays by Judith Duffey Harding, Eilean Hooper-Greenhill, Helen Joseph, Barbara Taylor,
featured artists: Jo Budd, Pauline Bainbridge, Dinah Prentice, Michele Walker
72pp, 25 col. illus.
ISBN 0 903261 42 1 (1998)

Contemporary Applied Arts, 50 Years of British Craft
Six essays ed. Tanya Harrod
published in association with CAA
88pp, 65 col. illus.
ISBN 0 9526267 5 6 (1998)

Eye of the Needle
the Textile Art of Alice Kettle
introduction by Dr Jennifer Harris
88pp, 70 col. illus.
ISBN 0 9526267 8 0 (1995)

all titles available from Telos
www. telos.net